Special Topics in Tarot

About Mary K. Greer

Mary K. Greer specializes in writing about and teaching methods of self-exploration and transformation. The author of six books on Tarot and a member of several Tarot organizations, she is featured at Tarot conferences and symposia around the United States and abroad. She has a wide following in feminist and pagan communities for her work in women's spirituality and magic. A priestess-hierophant in the Fellowship of Isis, she is founder of the Iseum of Isis Aurea.

Mary has studied and practiced Tarot and astrology for over thirty-five years. Her teaching experience includes eleven years at a liberal arts college and hundreds of workshops, conferences, and classes. She is the founder and director of the learning center T.A.R.O.T. (Tools And Rites Of Transformation). She coauthored the TarotL History Information Sheet.

About Tom Little

Tom Little is a health physicist at Los Alamos National Laboratory. He holds a Ph.D. in astronomy from New Mexico State University and has previously worked as a university professor and a technical writer. He is a Wiccan priest and serves on the board of Ardantane pagan learning center in northern New Mexico. Tom has used the Tarot as his primary spiritual tool for a number of years. He has a strong interest in Tarot history and antique decks, and has created extensive online resources for Tarot enthusiasts, including the Hermitage (a Tarot history site, www.tarothermit.com) and Tarot at Telperion Productions (www.telp.com/tarot/). He has coauthored and edited the TarotL Tarot History Information Sheet. He lives in Santa Fe, New Mexico.

Special Topics in Tarot

Understanding the
TAROT
COURT

MARY K. GREER
& TOM LITTLE

Llewellyn Publications
Woodbury, Minnesota

FIRST EDITION
Sixteenth Printing, 2022

Cover art © 2003 by Lauren O'Leary; background image © 2001 Photodisc
Cover design by Gavin Dayton Duffy
Project management by Jenny Gehlhar, Andrew Karre, and Rebecca Zins

Illustrations used by permission from the following decks:

Ancient Minchiate Etruria. Used with permission of Lo Scarabeo

Ancient Tarots of Marseille © Nicolas Conver. Used with permission of Lo Scarabeo

Golden Dawn Magical Tarot © Sandra T. and Chic Cicero / Llewellyn

The Pythagorean Tarot © John Opsopaus / Llewellyn

The Robin Wood Tarot © Robin Wood / Llewellyn

The Shining Tribe Tarot © Rachel Pollack / Llewellyn

Tarot Cards 1JJ. Used with permission of U.S. Games

Universal Waite Tarot. Used with permission of U.S. Games

World Spirit Tarot © Lauren O'Leary and Jessica Godino / Llewellyn

Tree of Life illustration on page 115 © Mary K. Greer

Library of Congress Cataloging-in-Publication Data
Greer, Mary K. (Mary Katherine)
   Understanding the tarot court / Mary K. Greer & Tom Little.—1st ed.
        p.   cm.
   Includes bibliographic references and index.
   ISBN: 978-0-7387-0286-5
   1. Tarot. I. Little, Tom, 1961-. II.Title.
   BF1879.T2G75 2004

   133.3'2424—dc22   2003065811

Llewellyn Publications
A Division of Llewellyn Worldwide Ltd.
2143 Wooddale Drive
Woodbury, MN 55125-2989
www.llewellyn.com
LLewellyn is a registered trademark of Llewellyn Worldwide Ltd.
Printed in the United States ofAmerica

Other Books by Mary K. Greer

Mary K. Greer's 21 Ways to Read a Tarot Card (Llewellyn, 2006)

Complete Book of Tarot Reversals (Llewellyn, 2002)

Tarot for Your Self, revised edition (New Page Books, 2002)

Women of the Golden Dawn (Park Street Press, 1995)

The Essence of Magic (Newcastle, 1993)

Tarot Mirrors (New Page Books, 1988)

Tarot Constellations (New Page Books, 1987)

Contents

Foreword

If you teach classes or workshops in Tarot, and you ask for questions, you will always get two questions among the rest. The first is "How do we read reversed cards?" and the second is "How do we interpret the court cards?" Mary Greer has come to our aid for the first with her truly *Complete Book of Tarot Reversals*, and now she and Tom Little, like true Tarot knights, have ridden to our rescue with this marvelous and thorough adventure in court card interpretation.

The reason why people have trouble with the court cards is really not a mystery. They just don't do all that much. The modern history of Tarot is largely a history of interpretation. Beginning in the last quarter of the twentieth century Tarot enthusiasts have sought to enter the pictures rather than have a standard set of formulaic meanings or a structural system to understand them. They will look at, say, the Five of Pentacles, and ponder what the people in the card are doing, where they are, what expressions they show and what body posture they hold, what might have happened to them in the past, what choices they might make in the future. All this then applies to the person who received the card in the reading and whatever question the person might have asked.

Until about a century ago this process was impossible, since the greater part of the deck, the forty pip cards (ace–ten in the four suits) showed no pictures at all, just elegant patterns of the suit emblems arranged on the card. In other words, the Six of Cups would not show any people or scene, just six elaborate cups in some sort of pattern, much the way we see the Six of Hearts in an ordinary playing card deck. This changed dramatically with the Rider-Waite-Smith deck, published in 1910. Working with the designer, Arthur Edward Waite, Pamela Colman Smith drew action scenes on all the pip cards. A sense of story entered the minor arcana, and story makes interpretation possible. Go to a movie with a friend and talk about it afterward, and you will discover how much opportunity story gives all of us to discover our own truths.

Along with the narrative quality of the pip cards, the trump cards, or major arcana, had always presented us with suggestions of complex symbolism. The court cards, however, were a problem. Until recently, the courts in most decks (the Thoth deck of Aleister Crowley and Frieda Harris was a notable exception) presented themselves in rather staid fashion. The kings and queens sat on their thrones, the knights charged on their horses, and the pages stood proudly holding their suit emblems.

In the older styles of Tarot reading, this formal quality of the courts actually worked rather well. This is because readers assumed that these cards referred to specific people, and you could identify those people with set formulas, such as age, sex, and hair and skin color. Such identification, however, is not the same as interpretation.

Greer and Little address the tradition that court cards refer to people. They consider it as one of the many possible ways to see these cards. Rather than just give us formulas, however, they come up with inventive and playful ways to figure out who the court figures might be. And they suggest methods so that we can sense if a card really does refer to a person, or one of the many other possibilities the book offers us.

Play is a hallmark of this book. Greer and Little know that when we play with images, ideas, possibilities, we give ourselves the chance to discover truth. And so, among many other techniques, we find an invitation to a "Tarot beach party." Later on, they show us how to create stories and screenplays out of Tarot cards, with the courts as a readymade cast of characters. I hope that someone does indeed film their script idea. It's a good one.

A good deal of the techniques in this book show the influence of the modern therapy movement, especially Jung and Perls. Just as Gestalt therapists tell their clients to see every thing in a dream (even inanimate objects) as them-selves, so Greer and Little tell us that "the single most powerful way" to view the court cards is as facets of the questioner's personality. This might be just a provocative idea if they did not also give us so many wonderful techniques. One of my favorites is the suggestion that we actually get the court cards in a reading to speak. Suppose you are using the Rider-Waite deck, and you get the Ten of Swords, the man with the ten swords sticking out of his back, and then the Knight of Wands. Can you imagine the knight coming across this scene? What would he do? What would he say about it? I happen to be writ-ing this on Arthur Conan Doyle's birthday, so my own impulse is to imagine the Knight of Wands as a detective, investigating the Ten of Swords crime scene. But that's just one version. Try it for yourself. And then consider that as an aspect of your personality and see what it tells you.

As well as ideas this book is simply filled with information. From Tarot history, to the wide range of correspondences in symbolic systems (indeed, it also contains a brief history of the very concept of correspondences), to a chart of the many court card variations in contemporary decks, they quite cover it all. After showing us all the ways we can discover our own mean-ings, they do give us the "traditional" meanings people have used for these cards—only, they do in so much virtuosic detail that it becomes yet another way to play with ideas.

So now, at last, we have an answer to a perennial question. From now on, when people in workshops ask "How do we interpret court cards?" I'll just hold up this book.

—RACHEL POLLACK

Acknowledgments

Would that I could acknowledge all the court cards in my life, but there are far more than sixteen of them, and more than I can mention here. First, I can hardly express the depth of my gratitude to all the people in my classes and workshops. Because of you many of these ideas have been created, tried, critiqued, and refined. I also want to thank those who make so many Tarot events possible: Geraldine Amaral, The Amberstones, Janet Berres, Jean-Michel David, the Omega Institute, Barbara Rapp, Valerie Sim, Thalassa, Glenn Turner, James Wells, and the publicity crew at Llewellyn for lending their support to our events. Special thanks to Barbara Moore at Llewellyn for her hard work and dedication to Tarot.

Many other Tarot professionals have added to my knowledge of the court cards: Fern Mercier, Rachel Pollack, Wald and Ruth Ann Amberstone, Tom Little, Jana Riley, and Linda Gail Walters, and the many fine Tarot authors and creators of Tarot decks. Thanks also go to members of all the Tarot e-groups for asking questions and sharing their ideas so freely.

My family is where I've learned most about the court card relationships: my mother, father and brothers, my daughters Casimira, Sierra and Jan, and Ed. The other major place where relationship dynamics both come alive and are consciously explored and nurtured is in the Symbols Group (what would

I do without you?): Charlotte, Chris, David, Jack, Kathryn, Lia, Sharyn, Vail, Virginia R., Virginia W. (in absentia), and Wylene. Special thanks go to Donna Hanelin to whom I personally dedicate this book.

—MARY K. GREER

I would like to acknowledge the Internet Tarot community as I found it when I first ventured into this fascinating study. I learned much in those first years of lively conversation, sharing, and debate. Although every voice was a part of the whole, I'll note just a few: Michele Jackson, Bob O'Neill, Mary Greer, Rachel Pollack, Alexandra Genetti, and the late Brian Williams.

I'm grateful to all the people at Llewellyn for their encouragement, support, and guidance at every stage of the process.

I owe a special and deep debt of gratitude to four friends for their personal and magical support on an almost daily basis during the time when this book was first conceived, written, and published: Diane Wilkes, Lori Cluelow, James Wells, and Ellen Lorenzi-Prince.

I dedicate this book to Anne-Marie, who has remained my center and my bedrock through many changes.

—TOM LITTLE

•

Introduction

The Tarot consists of seventy-eight cards divided into three sections—the twenty-two major arcana or trump cards; the forty pip or number cards, consisting of ace through ten in four suits; and the sixteen court cards, typically with a king, queen, knight, and page in each suit. This book is about interpreting the court cards in divinatory readings for yourself or others, and using them for personal guidance and self-understanding. You will also learn how to create your own court cards.

Divination can be defined as discerning, through a symbolic form of communication, how to come into harmony with the hidden forces of nature or the scheme of the universe. It leads to an understanding of fate as a character, and a revelation of the alchemical process by which we manifest our destiny, which is coming to know ourselves for who we truly are. The court cards depict sixteen different characters or personalities that are aspects of ourselves or aspects of others. The courts also serve as teachers, projections of our own unacknowledged qualities; they can represent events, stages, processes, and a variety of skills and abilities. They are divided into four suits that are most often called wands, cups, swords, and pentacles, which are usually equated in some way with the four elements: fire, water, air, and earth.

Court cards have traditionally featured characters from medieval courts. In recent years, however, designers have tried to move away from the courtly hierarchical structures and have substituted images associated with families, tribal life, and animals, among others. There are perhaps more substantive changes in the court cards than in any other part of the deck, making it impossible to set out definitive categorical interpretations that will work with every deck. Besides wanting to overthrow the hierarchy of the court, some deck creators have sought to overcome sexual stereotypes, ageism, and the racism inherent in an all-white, European cultural context. In some decks, the suits depict four different geographical regions, their races and cultures—a concept introduced by Antoine Court de Gébelin in the eighteenth century— while others depict elemental forces and entities. The titles for the cards likewise have changed so that the queen, for instance, has become lady, matriarch, woman, priestess, goddess, mother, guide, sibyl, lover, gift, or lodge.

Although we try to give examples of court cards from a variety of decks, we will emphasize traditional European decks and those with ideas derived from the Tarot system of the Hermetic Order of the Golden Dawn, which includes the Waite-Smith (also known as "Rider-Waite") and Thoth Tarot decks.

Court cards are generally considered the most difficult part of a Tarot deck to read and interpret. In fact, getting to know them is much like getting to know people—they start out as two-dimensional figures with simple defining characteristics, but can expand into richly complex personalities, styles, and events.

At the most basic, a court card would be interpreted as a person who has the characteristics of the suit, falls within a particular age range, and/or holds a certain rank within a family. Some readers might add an astrological sign, hair color, and specific sex to the description. If the card is upright, the individual has good intentions toward the querent; if reversed, the individual intends ill. In actual readings, such descriptions often fall far short of the full court card potentials. Sometimes no one fits the description, and other times it could indicate dozens of people. Who is the dark-haired, unmarried, youthful Taurus male Knight of Pentacles who is "crossing you" (a position in the Celtic Cross spread)? It might be obvious that it is someone at work who wants your job. But what happens when a busy fifty-five-year-old career woman, who has no children in her life, gets a Page of Cups in a position describing the "situation"? If you can't think of a person to whom it might refer, then tradition suggests that pages can refer to messages, and so, with cups, it could mean a love message. If this is not applicable, what does the Tarot reader suggest next? This book will provide you with many different possibilities.

As stated earlier, court cards are always about ourselves, but they can also represent other people, styles, or events. When they are reversed, we can discover where there are blocked energies and repressed gifts.

The purpose of this book is to make the court cards come alive, and to give you a deep familiarity with the cards and their possibilities. Before you begin, you should look over the definitions of important terms in appendix D. Check here whenever you are unsure about the meaning of a word or concept.

The Tarot Journal

This book is filled with examples and exercises. As you read through it, keep a deck, notebook, and pen or pencil at hand. Write down your impressions and experiences. You may also want to allocate several pages to each of the sixteen court cards so you can add important ideas, keywords, and interpretations under each card's name. If you are working with more than one deck, always indicate the deck you are using. Date your exercises because you may want to do some of them again later and will want to see how you've changed over time.

Your First Significator

One of the most familiar uses of the court cards in divination is the significator. The significator is a card that represents the querent—the person who is asking the question and about whom the reading is being done. Significators are chosen in many ways, which will be covered in chapter 1. Now is the opportunity for you to pick out a significator intuitively—without all the reasons that will be presented later. This way you can compare your own first impression with the results of later processes. Take your deck, and separate the sixteen court cards from the rest, laying them out faceup in a mixed grouping. Forget everything you know about these cards and simply look at the pictures.

1. Eliminate the cards that are least like you—getting rid of at least half. Keep these separate from the others.

2. Notice some of the characteristics that you used in the elimination process: Too old? Too young? Wrong color hair? Wrong sex? Overly harsh? Not friendly enough? Too dreamy? Too conservative? Interested in the wrong things?

3. From the cards that remain, does one card stand out clearly as being most like you? If not, examine the remaining cards in pairs, choosing one over the other by considering what you most connect with or where you see yourself most strongly. Then compare the chosen
card to a new card until only one is left. This is your significator.

4. From your initial stack of eliminated cards, find the card that is least like you. This could be called your "nemesis." It generally represents those characteristics you feel you were not allotted.

5. In your journal, write the ways in which you are most like your significator. Describe how your nemesis is not like you. One way to think of your nemesis is that if you were competing in this person's field, he or she would be an unbeatable rival; you could not possibly win. You may want to write down other cards that seemed to express a certain aspect of yourself that is noteworthy. Date your entries.

These "first impressions" will become more interesting and take on greater significance as you explore the court cards in depth.

In using this book you will establish a personal relationship with the court cards. By its conclusion, we hope you will have come to know and value the great diversity in human personality, and to view different needs and styles, within yourself and others, with compassion. This book works towards this goal by using established interpretive traditions as springboards for the imagination. Learning the court cards with this book is as much about creative play and searching out personal reactions to the cards as it is about studying established systems. The purpose of this book is to make the court cards come alive, and to give you a deep familiarity with the cards and the human possibilities they represent.

CHAPTER ONE

𝕿he Many Faces of the Tarot Court

The Tarot court cards represent four sets of royal couples with their retinues, each in their own domain, which, in playing cards, was marked by a heraldic device (which eventually became the suit emblem). In playing-card terminology, the court cards are also called royalty or face cards and, in seventeenth-century England, they were known as "coat cards" because of the elaborate coats or robes in which the figures were depicted. Some modern Tarot authors call them people cards in an effort to democratize them. In France and Italy, they are called *figura* or "figure" cards. Thus, the Tarot court are figures representing four different ranks of power and influence, in four different suits, elements, or domains. Since their heads or faces are usually prominent, and may be in profile or straight forward, the way they literally face can play an important part in interpretation.

There are many different ways to interpret the court cards. Determining which perspective is applicable in any given situation is part of the art of reading the cards. Most of this book is devoted to illuminating these different perspectives. Frequently more than one perspective will offer insights in the same reading, so it's good to get into the habit of scanning the possibilities.

In a reading, a court card may mean:

- A person in the your life, identified by his or her physical attributes, his or her profession, or the role he or she plays in the situation being examined (the Queen of Swords may represent a diplomatic, objective woman who acts as counselor or mediator, for example)

- An aspect of your personality, style or attitude, or a role you are playing (the Knight of Wands may express your impetuous, impulsive side)

- A relationship between the querent and another person (the Page of Pentacles is financially dependent on the king and so may represent dependency in a relationship)

- A spiritual influence at work in your life (the Knight of Cups may be a surge of emotional energy, producing excitement and romantic advances)

- An event or situation (the Page of Swords may be a message or piece of news about an important legal or business matter)

These interpretations of the court cards will be discussed in detail in subsequent chapters of this book. Other interpretations are possible as well. In fact, the possibilities are vast because the court cards have been interpreted in many different ways throughout the centuries. This book emphasizes interpretations that center on the idea of persona, whether one's own or that of another.

Suit and Rank

It is important to get to know the basic court figures and the terms we will be using for them in this book. The minor arcana cards are divided into four suits that usually correspond to the four elements. The court cards are divided into four ranks, originally indicating a relative position in society. The result is a 4 x 4 matrix of sixteen cards. However, the names, correspondences, and characteristics of suit and rank vary greatly from deck to deck. In some decks, especially pagan-oriented ones, wands (or batons) are associated with the element of air, while swords are fire. In the *Brotherhood of Light Egyptian Tarot*, coins (pentacles) are air, wands are earth, and swords are fire.

There are even a few rare decks where cups are air, and swords are water. This book will use the most common system, in which wands are fire and swords air, as its default, without intending for it to be seen as the only or best system. Feel free to use whatever elemental system you prefer.

Suits / Elements

WANDS / FIRE

The suit of wands is also known as batons, staves, rods, scepters, or clubs. Its element is fire, and it represents the desire for growth, and subsequently signifies: the inspiration that moves things, the desire that leads the way, the future-oriented aspiration that initiates action. Wands have a purpose behind every action, and find value primarily in the meaning of an experience while lacking appreciation for the form. Wands indicate the desire for self-growth and creativity. They want to expand awareness, as well as set everything on fire with their enthusiasm.

When you get a wands card, you might want to ask yourself: What has fired your interest? Do you have a burning desire to do something? Are you feeling burned out? Are you seeing red? What is erupting within you?

Wands generally signify:

• Projects	• Innovation	• Risk
• Energy	• Taking action	• Self-growth
• Spirit	• Inspiration	• Thesis
• Creativity	• Initiation	• Enthusiasm
• Desire	• Passion	• Perception
• Action	• Movement	• Optimism

CUPS / WATER

The suit of cups is also known as chalices, vessels, bowls, containers, or hearts. Its element is water, and water takes the form of whatever it flows into. Therefore cups are amiable but, at the same time, diffused. Cups represent going with the flow and seeking to merge. They receive the impulse from the fiery wands and respond to it. They represent love, relationship, and imagination, and provide nurturance and a sense of connectedness. Cups can open you to your inner feelings and the connections you have with others. Choices at this level seem instinctual.

When you get a cups card you might want to ask yourself: Am I going with the flow and where is it taking me? What emotions are flooding (drowning) me? Am I out of my depth? Am I all washed up? Am I being wishy-washy? Is this my cup of tea? What's coming in with the tide?

Cups generally signify:

• Feelings	• Heart	• Relationships
• Emotions	• Moods	• Unconscious
• Imagination	• Intuition	• Psychic powers
• Romance	• Dreams	• Visualization
• Receptivity	• Reflection	• Inner processes
• Mirroring	• Containment	• Sink-or-swim feelings

SWORDS / AIR

The suit of swords is sometimes known as blades, crystals, feathers, clouds, or spades. Its element is air, and it represents intellect, rationality, logic, analysis, and the actions that logically carry out these attributes. Swords dissect the original idea: they think about it, talk about it, struggle with it, organize it, and cut through anything not focused on the issue. Then they judge solely on reason and logic. Their methods often bring pain and sorrow, for anything that cannot stand the bright light of truth is ruthlessly cut away and destroyed. At the same time, swords thrive on the exchange and development of ideas, and, hence, communication. At their best they see all sides of an issue, weigh them carefully, and form clear, articulate opinions.

When you get a swords card, ask yourself: What's the point? Whom or what am I cutting off? Am I being sharp-tongued? What's clouding the issue? How can I clear the air? Am I throwing caution to the wind?

Swords generally signify:

• Conflict	• Thinking	• Law and order
• Criticism	• Analyzing	• Wit and cunning
• Strategy	• Planning	• Communication

• Struggle	• Discriminating	• Discussion
• Decisions	• Understanding	• Mental processes
• Reason	• Problem solving	• Fight-or-flight mechanism

PENTACLES / EARTH

The suit of pentacles is also known as coins, disks, stones, platters, or diamonds. Its element is earth, and it represents the fruits of your labor, the results of your history with other suits. At the same time, pentacles are the literal "ground" from which new ideas can grow. Pentacles make us feel secure by means of home, money, traditions, and control or power—all things we value and often receive in the form of rewards for the work we do. They give us an appreciation of form and of our bodies. With pentacles, we try to achieve mastery over matter, either through manual craft and skill, or through knowledge of how things work.

When you get a pentacles card ask yourself: What brings me down to earth? Am I being treated like dirt or the salt of the earth? Where's the diamond in the dust heap? What's steady as a rock? What will ground me? How can I stop being such a stick-in-the-mud?

Pentacles generally signify:

• Skills	• Value	• Grounding
• Worth	• Material	• Centeredness
• Tradition	• Security	• Health and fitness
• Sensation	• Results	• Physical, the body
• Actualization	• Fruits of labor	• Money and economics
• Manifestation	• Craftsmanship	• Rewards for accomplishment

Ranks

The ranks vary even more from deck to deck than the suits. The standard designations, which we will use in this book, are king, queen, knight, and page.

KING

The king depicts mature *yang*, or masculine energy. He shows outer, public mastery and expertise in his field. He is an authority figure, a commander, a manager, a minister, a person used to respect and obedience. He makes decisions and delegates tasks. He is in many ways like the Emperor of the major arcana, but with a focus and aptitude limited to the domain of his particular suit.

When you get a king, ask yourself: How do I express mastery, control, maturity, or integrity? Am I competent? Am I overbearing? Do I run things well?

Kings generally signify:

- Prowess
- Competence
- Mastery and leadership
- Authority
- Respect
- Decision making

QUEEN

The queen depicts mature *yin*, or feminine energy. She shows intra- and interpersonal mastery and expertise in her field. She leads by persuasion, by intuition, and by nurturing and encouraging others. She is a facet of the Empress, expressing understanding and creativity through the energy of her suit.

When you get a queen, ask yourself: How do I bring out the latent qualities in myself and others? Am I aware of subtleties? How do I nurture? What am I helping to form?

Queens generally signify:

- Understanding
- Persuasion
- Communication
- Teaching
- Nurturance
- Emotional awareness
- Creativity
- Intuition
- Leadership through consensus

KNIGHT

The knight depicts immature *yang*, or masculine energy. He lacks the king's sense of perspective but makes up for it in sheer energy. He can be brutally direct. He seeks to revolutionize and create change. He is the daring adventurer, the risk-taker, the romancer, the idealist. His essence is motion. He grasps his suit's lessons, however extreme they may be, by putting forth his all.

When you get a knight, ask yourself: What are my ideals? My obsessions? My goals and prizes? Do I know what I want? Am I relentless? Am I focused?

Knights generally signify:

- Energy
- Passion
- Motion toward a goal
- Intention
- Focus
- Single-mindedness
- Idealism
- Vitality
- Lust for life

PAGE

The page depicts immature *yin*, feminine or child energy. She is open, learning, curious, innocent, and ready to grow. The page loves life, receives it, and is immersed in the essence of the suit, living it out without complication. The page may also be a new person in your life, bringing messages and opportunities.

When you get a page, ask yourself: Am I ready to hear the message? Am I curious? Am I open to the stirrings of my dreams?

Pages generally signify:

• Curiosity	• Hope	• Innocence
• Opening	• Trust	• Beginnings
• Novelty	• Growth	• Study, apprenticeship

The Court Card Beach Party

Before looking at specific interpretations, here is a way to "break the ice" and get to know the court card personalities from your favorite deck. Pull out the sixteen court cards and lay them out in front of you in rows by suit and in columns by rank. You may want to tape the following guided visualization.

Find a comfortable position, take a couple of deep, cleansing breaths, and ground yourself in whatever way works for you. Imagine you are walking on a beach. Listen to the sound of the waves breaking along the shore. It is summer. The sand is pleasantly hot and there is a cooling breeze that makes the temperature comfortable. Feel the grains of sand under your feet, and the breeze against your face as you walk. Smell the fresh, tangy air. You hear the noise of a party in the distance, and soon come upon a group of people having a good time. They are the court cards and you suddenly remember that you were invited to this party.

As you approach them, the first person you see is someone who always makes you feel warm and welcome. You immediately feel appreciated and part of the group. Which card is this?

While talking to this court card you notice someone at a distance whom you don't like, who makes you feel uncomfortable, and who you will do anything to avoid. Which card is this?

You successfully avoid that person, but now notice someone you are physically attracted to, feeling drawn as if by a magnet. Which card is this?

Now you notice someone of any age who is goofing off like a kid and having a wonderful time. You feel lighthearted and playful just looking at this person. Which card is this?

Before you can join in the fun, you notice someone you deeply admire for his or her depth of wisdom and understanding. You can't miss this opportunity to be in his or her presence. Which card is this? Take a moment to find out what this figure has to say to you.

You feel an inner tug telling you it is time to return to your regular world, but first you look down at yourself and realize that you are a court card. Which card are you?

It is time to go, so walk back across the sand, away from the noise of the party, until the sound of the waves and wind fills your senses. Taking a deep breath, you quickly and easily find yourself back where you started, sitting in your room. You are fully present in your physical body and completely aware of your surroundings. Take another deep breath and, as you exhale, say your name to yourself three times as you open your eyes.

Take a moment to note why you picked each of the court cards above. What qualities of each figure made you feel as you did? Remember what the wise court card told you. Write down any impressions or memories of the experience in your Tarot journal.

Many Visions of the Tarot Court

Since the very beginnings of Tarot, designers have conceived of the court cards differently, using a variety of names for the ranks and altering their sex, age, and roles in society. Modern Tarot deck creators have experimented more freely with the court cards than with any other part of the deck.

The two most familiar court card systems, found in the Waite-Smith deck (reflecting the earlier Tarot de Marseille and historical decks) and the Crowley-Harris Thoth deck, are described in detail in the next chapter. Both of these systems have been enormously influential, and many modern decks follow their lead.

The Motherpeace Tarot, created by Vicki Noble and Karen Vogel, was one of the first decks to feature radically new court cards. They are called shaman, priestess, son, and daughter. Shamans represent power and experience. They have developed mastery and control over the qualities of their suit. Priestesses work from the heart. They receive and channel the energies and forces indicated by the suit, and are concerned with the sacredness of life. Sons have a light, playful quality. They use words and analysis, and they are focused and goal oriented. They represent the ego. Daughters are young and enthusiastic, representing the child within us all. They experience things through their senses and use wholistic thinking.

The Voyager Tarot, created by Jim Wanless and Ken Knutson, features the sage, child, woman, and man in order to point out two great dualities: masculine and feminine, and youth and age. These cards form what Wanless calls a "family of images" that work on both the inner and outer levels. Internally, they represent levels of self-mastery. When externalized, they are teachers or models of success or difficulties. The sage represents wisdom, know-how, and the expertise that comes from experience. The child represents new growth and learning, exploration, spontaneity, openness, and curiosity. The woman or mother card stands for our receptive, feeling qualities. She is introspective and self-aware, sensitive, nurturing and people oriented. The man or father card is the revolutionary. He is externally directed, action and goal oriented. He seeks change and desires to transform things.

The World Spirit Tarot, by Lauren O'Leary and Jessica Godino, features the sage, sibyl, seeker, and seer. They describe each of the court or "people" cards as a "character sketch":

> The seers are students, curious about the world around them. They are young and delicate, and need nurturance and protection. Seekers interact more dynamically with the world, questing for answers and challenges, taking risks, and trying to get things done. As young adults they lack experience and maturity, but not enthusiasm. The sibyls are the mature embodiment of their suit. They use their energies wisely and know how to govern their realms with ease. The sages are accomplished in the world. They bring a broad perspective garnered by age and responsibility, and they possess great authority.[1]

The cups court cards from the World Spirit Tarot

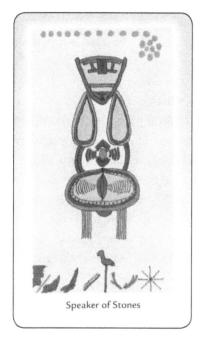

Speaker of Stones

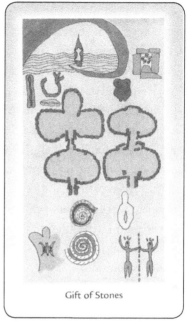

Gift of Stones

Knower of Stones

Place of Stones

The stones vision cards from the Shining Tribe Tarot

The Shining Tribe Tarot, created by Rachel Pollack, introduces us to "vision cards" called place, knower, gift, and speaker. They do not represent character types, but instead, as Pollack says, "take us into an experience of ourselves" and demonstrate how to understand and use the power of each element. The place cards depict a location and concrete image, revealing what each suit and its qualities can give. Pollack describes the knower as "the mythic champion of each suit. It gives us a feeling for what it would mean to understand and experience those elemental qualities . . . [and] who we might become if we embodied them." The gift cards recall emblems of the four suits, and we learn to truly appreciate their powers. They "help us recognize the gifts we receive [from Spirit] . . . [through] amazing experiences or a special helper or teacher." The speakers remind us that our actions come from a power within ourselves. They speak or act with authority and confidence and have "the responsibility to share elemental power with others and serve the greater community."

The Cosmic Tarot, created by Norbert Lösche, melds the Waite-Smith and Thoth systems with court cards titled king, queen, prince, and princess, and imagery drawn from movie stars. Similarly, the *Victoria Regina Tarot*, by Sarah Ovenall, titles the court cards as king, queen, prince, and princess, but the images depict well-known public figures from Victorian England.

The summary chart that follows illustrates the range of variation in court card systems but is not meant to be all-inclusive. Most decks that are not mentioned in the chart probably use either the Waite-Smith or Thoth court card titles.

COMPARISON CHART OF THE COURT CARD RANKS

	King	Queen	Knight	Page
Standard English (RWS, Marseilles, etc.)	King	Queen	Knight	Page
Antique Italian	Re	Regina	Cavaliere	Fante
Papus (French)	Roi	Dame	Cavalier	Valet
Balbi (Spanish)	Re	Reina	Caballo	Sota
Golden Dawn	King	Queen	Prince	Princess
Thoth	Knight	Queen	Prince	Princess
Adams' Parrott[a]	King	Queen	Mentor Prince	Princess
Alchemical	King	Queen	Knight	Lady
Knapp/Hall	King	Queen	Warrior	Servant
Celtic Wisdom	King	Queen	Warrior	Woman
Merryday	King	Queen	Warrior	Elemental
Xultun Mayan	Lord	Lady	Warrior	Servant
Native American	Chief	Matriarch[c]	Warrior	Maiden
Quester	Patriarch	Matriarch	Warrior	Maiden
Storyteller	Master	Mistress	Warrior	Novice
Shapeshifter	God	Goddess[c]	Warrior	Seeker
Inner Child	Guardian	Guide	Seeker	Child
William Blake	Man	Woman	Angel	Child
Voyager	Sage	Woman	Man	Child
World Spirit	Sage	Sibyl	Seeker	Seer
Dance of Life	Sage	Lover	Dancer	Muse
Songs for the Journey Home	Resolving	Creating	Awakening	Innocence
Shining Tribe	Speaker	Gift	Knower	Place
New Orleans Voodoo	Houngan	Mambo	La Place	Hounsis
Medicine Woman	Exemplar	Harvest Lodge	Totem	Apprentice
Greenwood[b]	King	Queen	Knight	Page
Tarot of the Spirit	Father	Mother	Brother	Sister
Elemental	Father	Mother	Son	Daughter
Vision Quest	Father	Mother	Son	Daughter
Motherpeace	Shaman	Priestess	Son	Daughter
Amazon	Companion	Queen	Amazon	Child

Tarot of the Crone	Shadow	Grandmother	Witch	Beast
Daughters of Moon	Crone		Mother	Maiden
Baseball		Coach	MVP	
Qabalistic[d]	Yod (Vav)	Heh	Vav (Yod)	Heh Final
Elements[d]	Fire (Air)	Water	Air (Fire)	Earth

Several decks feature court cards from different ethnic and cultural groups and historical periods, often using a different one for each suit:

	wands	*cups*	*swords*	*pentacles*
Tarot of the Ages	Central Africa	Central America	Northern Europe	India
Kazanlar	India (Moguls)	Hungary	Persia	Egypt
Ancestral Path	Egypt (19th dynasty)	Arthurian Britain	Feudal Japan	Post-contact North America
Haindl	India	Celtic countries	Egypt	North America
Court de Gébelin[e]	Southern countries	Northern countries	Orient	Occident

FOOTNOTES FOR ABOVE CHARTS

a   The *Parrott Tarot* (published by SS Adams Co.) has five court cards: "the Mentor is not necessarily a person. He or she is a 'teacher' or 'lesson' which could come from a book, an experience, a process, or a human being"[from the accompanying booklet].

b   While the *Greenwood Tarot* has traditional names for the court cards, the figures are all animals.

c   The creators of these decks specified that these cards are the highest in the Tarot court—a position usually held by the king.

d   For purposes of this book, the consort of the water queen is considered to be fire, and the card paired with the earth page is considered to be air.

e   Antoine Court de Gébelin did not design a deck, but, having given the first account of an occult Tarot, he influenced future decks.

Court Cards As Significator

One of the primary uses of court cards in a reading is as the significator of the querent. It serves as a sign or token of that person's identity and presence, a proxy in cardboard, existing at the same level of symbolic reality as the cards providing the response. It serves as witness to your intent to derive meaning from what you see.

The significator can also represent the intent or purpose of the reading or the subject of your concern, rather than the person being read for.

Of course, any one of the seventy-eight cards can be used, but traditionally the significator is one of the sixteen court cards.

Choosing the Significator

The most basic method for choosing your significator is by sex, age, physical description, and/or sun sign as indicated in the chart below. However, physical description based on European standards of eye and hair color is not relevant to the majority of people on this planet. If you are doing phone or e-mail readings, it involves asking rude and unnecessary questions. You can always take these characteristics into consideration without making them your only criteria.

SUITS

Wands: Fire signs. Blond to red hair. Blue or hazel eyes.

Swords: Air signs. Brown hair. Brown eyes.

Cups: Water signs. Light brown hair. Blue, brown, or hazel eyes.

Pentacles: Earth signs. Brunette or black hair. Blue or hazel eyes.

RANKS

Queens: Mature or married woman.

Kings: Mature or married man.

Knights: Young unmarried man.

Pages: Child or young unmarried woman.

Some readers prefer to choose a significator based on wider meanings ascribed to the court cards. The exercises throughout this book will provide you with a range of associations that can be used to connect a person with a particular court card.

Another way to choose significators is the intuitive method. All sixteen court cards are laid out for the querent to contemplate and then choose spontaneously the card with which he or she most identifies at the moment. This has the benefit of alerting the reader to how the querent perceives him- or herself.

A fourth technique is for the querent to randomly select a card from either the whole deck or just the court cards. This method gives the reader information about which aspect of the querent is asking the question or an additional hint of what the question is really about.

Selecting a Significator at Random

A quick method for drawing a court card at random is to shuffle, cut, and restack the deck, and then turn over cards from the top of the deck until the first court card appears. This is your significator for this spread. Reshuffle the cards for the reading itself. Alternatively, lay out the cards in the spread first, and then continue to draw cards until a court card appears. (The intervening cards are not used.) To select any card from the deck for a significator, shuffle the deck, spread the cards facedown in a fan, and select one.

Further Work with Significators

You can leave your significator in the deck. Some people feel that when a card with which they strongly identify appears randomly in a spread, it marks that reading as especially important. The whole spread is *accidentally dignified*. For example, one man was involved in extensive inner-child work and had begun identifying himself with the curiosity of the Page of Wands. Whenever this card appeared in a spread, he knew immediately that the reading referred to the psychological work he was doing and the material he was reclaiming from his childhood. When reading for a querent, unless he or she makes a point of informing the Tarot reader of the importance of such a card, these personal observations may be totally overlooked.

The Golden Dawn uses an interesting technique in which the significator is selected (traditionally based on physical or astrological characteristics—although any method may be used) and then shuffled back into the deck. The cards are prepared for the reading (usually all seventy-eight cards were dealt into the spread) and the significator sought (while maintaining the order of the cards). The location of the significator indicates one or more of the following:

- A set of cards to be interpreted (a house in a zodiac spread or pile of cards after a cut)—all other sections are ignored
- The beginning of the reading (cards prior to the significator are ignored)
- The "present point" that divides past from future (the significator "faces" the future and away from the past, or cards dealt prior to the significator are in the past and the ones after it are in the future)

In most spreads, choosing a significator is optional or, at least, nonessential. Many people prefer not to have a particularly important card removed from the possibility of appearing in the reading. A few decks have extra cards that are either blank, give the deck title, or carry a design. Any of these can be used as permanent significators. *The Kazanlar Tarot* provides two cards just as significators: a Persian-garbed male and a European-garbed female. In the *Ancestral Path Tarot*, created by Julie Cuccia-Watts, the Fool card was specifically designed to represent the inquirer. The picture shows the Fool with a Tarot card in her hand and a mirror behind her.

The significator is a point of focus or concentration. Since all other cards in a reading refer back to the significator as the subject of the reading, this can be either helpful or limiting, depending on the issue and how broad the information is that you are seeking.

For example, a thirty-year-old woman wants to know what would happen if she went back to school. She selects the Page of Pentacles to represent herself as a dedicated student, plus she, like the page, has black hair and is unmarried. When both the Five of Swords and the King of Swords (a critical teacher or inner critic) turn up in the reading, they seem to overwhelm the Page of Pentacles, pointing to a level of stress and critical attack that could be devastating.

Alternately, the same woman picks the Queen of Swords for her significator since she has a Libra sun sign and is well past adolescence. Now the Five of Swords and King of Swords seem to indicate mental sparring that could be easily handled by a well-matched partner.

The choice of significators theoretically would determine the cards that turn up in the spread, but if the woman always chooses the Page of Pentacles or Queen of Swords as her significator, then only these aspects of herself will ever be explored.

Some readers prefer to use a significator when it is a functional part of the spread.

Consider the following statements:

- I always see myself as a particular court card and find it hard to imagine that anyone else would fit this card as well.

- I can't imagine removing any card from the possibility of appearing in the spread.

- When cards with which I most identify appear randomly in the spread, I feel that the reading is trying to tell me something especially important.

- When I think of myself, I primarily see my physical appearance.

- When I think of myself, I primarily see my psychological characteristics.

- When I think of myself, I primarily see my familial, social, or business positions.

Which ones do you most agree with? Which ones are not true for you? What do your responses suggest about how you might want to select and use significators in your own practice?

Significator Exercise

Pick a significator to represent yourself, shuffle all seventy-eight cards (including your significator), making sure that cards are randomly reversed. Deal cards off the top of the deck, turning them faceup as you do so. When you get to your significator, lay out in a line the two cards that came before the significator and then the two cards that came after it. Determine what direction the significator is facing. (If the significator is facing straight ahead and upright, treat it as facing right; if it is reversed, then treat it as facing left.) The nearest card in the direction faced is your next action and the farther card is a result of that action. Looking in the other direction, the nearest card is what brought you into the present, the farther card is what prompted that. Read the cards using the techniques suggested below. (All other cards may be read as upright if you don't normally use reversals.)

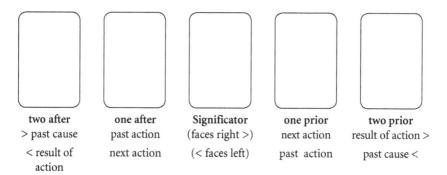

two after	one after	Significator	one prior	two prior
> past cause	past action	(faces right >)	next action	result of action >
< result of action	next action	(< faces left)	past action	past cause <

How to Read a Card

Throughout this book, when you are reading the cards or are asked to describe what you see in a card, you are encouraged to use the following process. Although, with practice, the process of taking in the full importance of the card's imagery can become quicker and more automatic, it is a good idea to become familiar with this process before simplifying or bypassing it. Each step makes a distinctive contribution to the final interpretation.

1. Say the name of each card out loud. Sounds simple, but people sometimes stare at a card without knowing what to say or where to begin.

2. Think of one to three keywords for its rank and suit, or a phrase summing up the qualities of that particular card.

3. Simply describe the card—literally and concretely. Don't worry about meanings and interpretations. In fact, try to be as objective as possible. Simply describe what you see. For instance, for the Waite-Smith

Queen of Pentacles, "A woman is sitting on a stone chair. It is carved with fruit and a goat's head. There are red roses on branches above her head. She wears a red robe over a white undergarment. . . ." Be as specific and detailed as you can without making any assumptions about what is happening or what anything means.

4. Repeat everything you just said but this time in the first person, present tense. "I am sitting on a stone chair with fruit and a goat head carved on it. I am wearing . . ." This allows you to clarify your impressions, check the details, add a few if necessary, but more especially, note which ones stand out because they relate to or remind you of something in your own life.

5. Next, what seem to be the feelings, attitudes, and emotions of the figure(s) in the card? Also, what seem to be the mood and atmosphere of the environment? For instance, "The woman seems to be contemplating the object in her lap; she looks sad or pensive although it is a warm, bright day. There is also a rabbit that appears playful and unafraid."

6. Repeat everything you just said—in the first person, present tense, again. More than one thing in the picture may represent you. For instance, you could be the rabbit in the Queen of Pentacles and the queen herself. "I am contemplating something in my lap. I feel sad and pensive although it is a warm, bright day. Another part of me is playful and unafraid." See what happens when you use the first person to refer to yourself as an inanimate object or even the atmosphere—are they parts of yourself, or of the environment around you? "Although I generally seem warm and bright, I am feeling sad and pensive about this thing I hold."

7. Turn some of your statements into questions ("Although I generally feel good, what am I most pensive about?") and answer them.

8. Spontaneously make up a fairy tale about what is happening in the card. Imagine the card is an illustration in a children's book, catching just one moment of the story. Tell what came before and after the scene depicted in the card. Be wild and outlandish. Your story can

go anywhere; the characters can do anything. Don't think, just talk or write for three minutes. Begin your story with "Once upon a time . . ."

9. Repeat this story in the first person, present tense.

10. You can also physically assume the position of the figure on the card. Be as accurate as possible. Imagine you are in that environment. What are you doing, thinking, and wanting? How do you move? What do you say? Of whom, or what, does this scenario remind you?

11. How does all this relate to your life right now? Describe any circumstances that come to mind, and make associations as you go. Is this truly yourself or does it seem more like someone else you know? This step may come at any point and be repeated as necessary.

If you are reading for someone else, you can describe the card and then turn parts of the descriptions that you've intuitively deemed important into statements or questions for the querent. However, try guiding the querent through the above process while you listen closely to what the querent says. You'll know when they've touched on something vital. Ask for clarification or more details to help the querent go deeper or be more specific. You can also repeat what he or she has said when it is clear the querent should pay special attention. You'll often hear people answer their own questions, long before they realize the significance of what they've said.

How You'd Like to Be Seen

In this exercise you will choose a court card that represents how you would like to see yourself. Begin by jotting down at least five qualities that you have and take pride in. Reflect on whether others recognize, acknowledge, and appreciate these qualities in you. If the quality is not as apparent to others as you would like it to be, underline it.

Now think of at least five positive qualities that you would like to develop and exhibit more. At present, do not list negative qualities you feel you might have. (For example, instead of thinking, "I'm too shy," say, "I'd like to be more outgoing," and write down "outgoing" as a quality you would like to develop in yourself.) Underline two or three of these qualities that you feel are especially important.

Now go through the court cards of your deck and find the one that best embodies the qualities you have listed, paying special attention to the underlined ones. This is your "ideal self" card.

Compare the card you chose with your significator and nemesis cards. (It should be different from both of them, because it represents both qualities you feel you have and qualities you feel you do not have.) What do your significator and your ideal-self card have in common? (Are they the same suit, the same rank, the same gender?) How are they different? Is your ideal self more mature or more youthful? Does your ideal self share any qualities with your nemesis?

Imagine your significator card interacting with your ideal-self card. What is their relationship? How does your ideal-self card make your significator feel—defensive, adulatory, amicable, uneasy, competitive? How would your significator have to change to become like your ideal-self card? What would have to be given up?

Think of one specific situation in your life where you have the opportunity to act more like your ideal-self card, and imagine what concrete steps you could take to seize this opportunity. Note this in your journal, then give it a try and see what happens!

ENDNOTES

1   Jessica Godino and Lauren O'Leary, *The World Spirit Tarot*, pp. xv–xvi.

CHAPTER TWO

The Court Card Family

We can read volumes about the lives of our friends and acquaintances by observing nuances of facial expression and body language and by noting how our friends behave with others. Likewise, by closely examining the visual details on Tarot court cards, you will discover personalities and relationships, especially when a group of cards are studied together. The court cards of a single suit can be seen as forming a natural "family" or "household," an intimate little cluster of personalities that we may study in order to practice our people-watching skills. Each deck offers its own variation on family dynamics.

Seeing the Family in the Court

Let's look at the *Minchiate Etruria* deck, an antique deck from eighteenth-century Florence. Having ninety-seven cards, there are more major arcana than in a modern Tarot deck, but the minor arcana are the familiar fifty-six, and the court cards are unusually expressive. We have no "book meanings" from the designer of the deck to rely on, but very distinct personalities can be assigned to each card—keep in mind conventional suit and rank associations, note how the figures are depicted, and imagine how they would interact living under the same roof. Here, we'll examine the *Minchiate Etruria* cups family. This is but one example of conclusions that can be drawn from the viewing the cards imaginatively. You may find that you see them in a very different way.

King of Cups

Queen of Cups

Knight of Cups

Handmaiden of Cups

The four cups court cards from the Minchiate Etruria Tarot

This is the suit of hearth and home, family relationships, emotional bonds, and the like. These figures are happier than the batons family, but not without their subtle tensions and conflicts.

Even in the old Tarots, some of the court card figures seem to convey a consistent personality across a wide range of decks. Two such recurring themes are the King of Cups as a friendly, if unambitious, grandpa-like character, and the Knight of Cups as a disreputable person, perhaps a manipulator or user of sorts. There is also an aura of hedonism surrounding the cups, especially the male figures.

King of Cups

He's almost a Santa Claus, with his caring expression and receptive pose. Seen as an authority figure in matters of love and family, his role is neither complex nor burdensome. He offers friendly support, performs fatherly rituals, and passes on his favorite childhood stories to the grandkids. Family life doesn't require any more of an "authority figure" than this. He has lots of free time, which he devotes to creature comforts: wine, music, conversation, perhaps gardening or tending to the dogs and horses. He is probably the most passive, most docile, most friendly of the kings—far more so than the equivalent Waite-Smith depiction.

He is the kind elder, the sympathetic counselor, the tolerant parent, or the retiree, enjoying his life of leisure.

Queen of Cups

In many decks, the Queen of Cups is a fountain of love: pure, giving, and thoroughly empathic and intuitive. In this deck, the Queen of Cups seems to take a much more active stance. She's the matron of the house, the organizer, the manager, and perhaps something of a busybody. Whereas the king has little to do, except dandle the grandkids on his knee, the queen has the formidable task of keeping the household operating smoothly, day in and day out. She's constantly giving direction to the servants, and making sure that none of the family members step out of line or disrupt the appearance of a happy home. We wonder if she's ever pushed past her limits, but she seems to have tremendous reserves of strength and a good feeling for how relationships work. She keeps her sanity through delegating and imposing a dense net of behavioral expectations to which others must conform.

She is the domestic organizer, the chaperone or matchmaker, setting rules for interpersonal conduct. As a source of stability in family matters, she mediates among family members to diffuse tensions.

Knight of Cups

This is one of the most interesting cards of the Minchiate deck. He has the upper body of a man, but the lower body of a sea griffin. He points to his cup with an expression of mock innocence. Sea griffins seem to be much more popular in heraldry than in literature, and it is not easy to find references that would shed some light on his personality. (It is recorded, however, that griffin's claws were sold as a way to detect poisons. Think twice before drinking from that cup.)

If the knights represent incursions of our bestial nature into the domain of human society, then the Knight of Cups offers a treasure trove of hidden impulses. His wings suggest flight and emotional expression, through poetry and the arts, and the intense ecstasy of love. His body and claws are earthy, acquisitive, and strong. He can be outrageously possessive and boldly aggressive. His serpentine tail suggests the murky deeps of the subconscious, filled with inner turmoil and unarticulated needs. Altogether, it paints a strong picture of all the animal desires that enter into our need to form relationships with others. His human half is hardly a match for all that. At best, he maintains a superficially civilized persona.

He is, no doubt, an acute embarrassment to the Queen of Cups, who gave birth to this monstrosity of an emotional predator. He is obsequious in her presence, but that just makes it worse, because his duplicity makes it impossible for her to control him.

He is the keeper of amorous obsessions, artistic and creative passions, possessiveness and manipulation in relationships. He symbolizes the extremes of the heart: lust, jealousy, despair.

Handmaiden of Cups[1]

This young girl is a housemaid, apparently severely overworked. When the queen delegates, she delegates to the maid. The maid cleans up when the king falls asleep amidst empty bottles, she helps camouflage the knight's excesses, and she keeps all the plates and glasses filled. For all this, she receives hardly any appreciation. The queen is a perfectionist, always worried that some cracks will show in the family's polished image—and the maid never quite lives up to her expectations. Nevertheless, her devoted service is what keeps the family functioning. Too bad she's too busy to benefit from it!

She represents devoted service to friends and family, being on the giving end of an unbalanced relationship, taking care of practical details on behalf of loved ones, and attending to household chores.

General Observations

In the feminine suits of cups and coins, in this deck the women have the true power, and the men, although deferred to as a formality, are actually dependent on the women. Thus the men have a certain opportunity for luxury and self-indulgence that the women cannot afford. This is certainly true with the King of Cups, who has the most pleasant and uncomplicated relationships with his loved ones because his paternal role is supported by the hard work of the queen and handmaiden. The knight can wallow in his inner turmoil, again thanks to a support system that mitigates the consequences of his excess. This all takes its toll on the queen and maid, who are never able to relax or thoroughly enjoy the relationships they work so intently on sustaining. All these roles fit together into a stable, if somewhat dysfunctional, family environment.

Later in this chapter, there is an exercise in which you describe the court card families of your own deck.

A Family Affair

In most Tarot decks, the court card figures are a mature man and woman (king and queen) and two younger people (knight and page). Thus, the tendency is to see the court as a nuclear family of parents and children. These relationships are made explicit in some decks, where the cards have titles such as father, mother, brother, sister, son, daughter, prince, princess.

The family is a succinct and powerful distillation of the world of human interaction. For most of us, the family provides our earliest formative experiences of others and sets the stage for all future relationships. It is in the family that we first learn about love, conflict, authority, cooperation, and responsibility. It is where we acquire our first masks, taking on roles in response to the expectations of others. Family relationships can be varied and complex. They differ from society to society, and each family is unique. Yet, in the court cards of the Tarot, this complexity is distilled into pictorial figures that encapsulate the dynamics of a family or household. Much of the landscape of our childhood roles, for example, is to be found in the rebellious, energetic knight, and the receptive, eager-to-please page. And parents, regardless of gender, may find themselves drawn toward the commanding figure of the king or the understanding, conciliatory energy of the queen.

Growing Up: A Spread

This spread is an example of using the Tarot for retrospective contemplation, not to predict future events but to see the past in a clearer light. It is especially useful for revisiting the challenges of childhood and matters of early family life. Find a court card to represent yourself as you are at present. You may use the significator you chose in the introduction or in chapter one, or pick another card. It is especially appropriate to use one of the "mature" court cards (a queen or king) in this spread. Now pick a second card to represent yourself as a child. Pages are an obvious choice, but a knight can also be appropriate. The two cards might be of the same suit, but need not be. Place these cards at positions 1 (your child self) and 5 (your present self) of the spread, and then shuffle the remaining cards of the deck.

Then deal cards into positions 2, 3, and 4.

- Position 2 represents an important trigger or stimulation in your maturation: an event or person who prompted you to leave childhood behind and find your adult self.

- Position 3 is the core issue of your growing-up process: the reality you had to grapple with and master in order to become who you now are. If there is a court card in this position, it can represent an intermediate stage of development, a persona you had to master to leave childhood behind.

- Position 4 is an alternative possibility, somewhere your life might have taken you if you had made different choices in dealing with the issue presented by card 3.

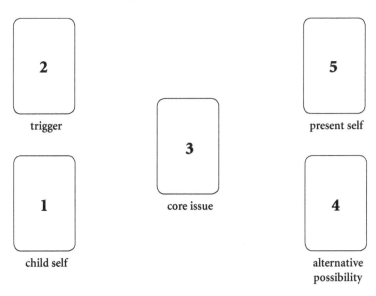

"Growing up" is not something that happens during adolescence and then is over with; this spread can reveal transformations that have occurred later in life, or that are still in process. You may want to try this spread to look at how your own parents "grew up"—we often see our parents as permanent adults (queens and kings of the court), but they were once children too.

The Waite-Smith and Thoth Court Card Systems

Different decks have used the model of a family in different ways in order to draw attention to various kinds of relationships and roles, or to conform to a metaphysical system.

In the late nineteenth century, the Hermetic Order of the Golden Dawn associated the elements, not just with the suits, but also with the ranks. The page was the fruition of earth and the queen was emotional water. The knight on his horse was the dynamic and initiating force of fire. However, since fire and water are the primary elements, this meant that knight and queen were natural consorts. The knight was promoted to king (they hand-wrote it on their cards), while the former king was demoted to son or prince and associated with the air element. The page was the daughter, called princess, in order to achieve a desired gender balance.

Both A. E. Waite (creator of the Waite-Smith Tarot deck, with artist Pamela Colman Smith) and Aleister Crowley (co-creator of the Thoth deck, with artist Frieda Harris) were members of the Golden Dawn. Waite followed standard Tarot tradition in making the king the highest ranking card in the court. Crowley followed the Golden Dawn, but retained the rank-name knight for the consort of the queen, making the knight the highest station and demoting the king to prince. The difference, it seems, expresses fundamentally different views of the world. In the traditional system used in Waite's deck, the competence and objectivity of the dignified, enthroned king were paramount. For Crowley, it was the dynamic (and sexual) energy of the knight that was most important. This difficult contrast in perspectives will be discussed in more depth later. When we discuss the elemental associations of the court card ranks later in this book, we will make the simplifying assumption that the consort of the queen (whether called knight, king, or something else) is associated with the element of fire. However, with many decks (including the Waite-Smith), the deck's creator did not make such correspondences explicit, and other interpretations are possible.

What is the family model found in decks that use king, queen, knight, and page—like the Tarot de Marseille and the Waite-Smith deck? These ranks are at home in a royal household of Europe's feudal period. This was a patriarchal society. The king was absolute ruler of his domain, which he inherited from his father. His consort, the queen, likely entered into the family to secure a political alliance, consolidate land, or because of her potential to produce a strong son and heir to the throne. The knight might be simply one of the king's military commanders or ambitious young vassals, but he might also be the son and heir to the throne, proving his prowess in tournaments and battles. He may be energetic and rebellious, but his rebellion is safely compartmentalized as "youthful vigor." After having had his adventures, he will one day dismount from his horse and settle into his father's throne, becoming the symbol and executor of the status quo. The page would be their household servant or foster child, probably not related to them, but still living with them and attending to their needs.

Many elements of this model of a household are still embedded deeply in our culture. Even as we live in nontraditional families or work with less authoritarian parenting models, the figure of the father as "lord of his castle" and the unambiguous chain of command from father to mother to teen to child still evokes powerful cultural expectations and personal reactions.

In the Thoth Tarot, the primary couple is the knight and the queen, and their son and daughter are respectively called the prince and princess. The Golden Dawn applied the name king to the figure on horseback, while the former king was called prince or emperor and was depicted riding in a chariot. Crowley's variation drew on the following conception of the pagan cultures of prepatriarchal Europe and Egypt.

Once upon a time, communities were so isolated they became genetically inbred, lessening vigor and fertility. Because the rulers were often seen as gods, their health and well being were linked directly to that of the land and to the entire community. As a king became old and infertile, or was injured (like the Fisher King in the Grail legends), the land would dry up and become a wasteland, or the king would be unable to vanquish a ravaging monster. And so it came to pass that new blood (and genetic material) was needed to revivify the royal lineage, which was passed down through the queens. When a strange knight rode into town, he faced a test to determine his strength and wisdom. He had to vanquish a dragon or a sphinx, solve a riddle, save a maiden, or obtain a rare object. Often his actions would result in the death of the old king. If he succeeded in his tasks, he was given the hand of the queen in marriage. The son of their union was the prince, in training to be king. The princess, their daughter, represented the fertile potential of the people and the continuance of the lineage, while the queen mother represented the royal throne or the land itself.

The Thoth system thus presents a very different family dynamic, one in which the men lead and rule by virtue of their relationships with the women, who represent the lineage and sovereignty of the land and its people. This knight is more powerful and masterful than the traditional knight, taking on many of the qualities of the traditional king, yet retaining the vitality and drive of the traditional knight. The knight must prove himself worthy of being brought into the bloodline, ironically reversing the way women were married into patriarchal lineages in the feudal model, and instead preserving the matriarchal way women were married according to fairy tales and folklore. The actual business of rulership, which is assigned to the king in feudal-model decks and thus equated with ultimate authority, is assigned to the prince in the Thoth deck. This makes rulership a secondary value in comparison with the knight's heroism and sexuality. The prince, which Crowley also called an emperor, must be set in motion by his father and mother. The Thoth princess brings out feminine potential rather than the childlike subservience of the traditional page. She is in some ways the most important figure of the four, because she represents permanence and continuity. Through her, the royal lineage survives into the next generation, and so the kingdom survives as well. So in the Thoth system, each court figure wields a distinctive and crucial kind of power, and the whole system is kept in dynamic equilibrium by the complementary roles of male and female.

It is important to understand that the Thoth system differs from the Waite-Smith system not merely in the names of the court cards, but in the relationships among them. There is no way to equate the cards from one system with those of the other so that they signify the same thing.

Some of the other decks mentioned in chapter one extend the concept of family by introducing figures representing elders, spiritual leaders, or even abstractions. The nuclear family is only one resource for interpreting the Tarot court cards. Contemporary family arrangements often do not conform to the mold of father/mother/son/daughter. Many households do not have children at all. There are single parents, same-sex marriages and partnerships, and grandparents who assume traditional parental roles. It is an interesting exercise to contemplate what the Tarot court would look like if it were patterned on your own household (either the one you were raised in or the one you are living in now).

Exercise: The Court As Household

Take the four court cards of one suit from your deck (pick any suit that interests you) and place them in front of you.

- Pay attention to their age, physical appearance, demeanor, facial expression, and body language.

- Visualize them as a household. How do they treat each other?

- Do they function well as a team, or are there problems?

- Can you tell who is in charge? How?

- Is there a scapegoat or black sheep?

- If there are cards corresponding to a king and queen, what is their relationship? What is the balance of power between them?

- If there is a knight or prince, is he their son, or is he their vassal?

- If there is a page or princess, is she or he subservient? A family member, or not?

- Does the group have any "collective personality" that you can detect?

- If you were a living in their world, what feelings might you have toward them as a group?

There's no need to meditate deeply on each card, just make mental note of your "first impressions." Try to set aside anything you might know about the cards from previous Tarot experience and simply see them as pictures of people. Imagine they are in a television soap opera or a fairy tale. There are no wrong answers. Write a description of this "family."

The Four Modes of Tarot

What makes the court cards different from the other cards in the deck? The seventy-eight-card Tarot deck consists of four different segments or "modes," and each has a unique role to play in interpretation. By drawing one card from each group, you can discover how each of these modes is operating in your life and, at the same time, get a feel for how they operate in their own unique way in any reading.

Court Cards

These answer the question "Who?" They show what part of yourself (or another), from among sixteen sub-personalities—masks and personas—is involved in the situation. How are you acting? What role are you playing?

Minor Arcana Number Cards (2 through 10)

These answer the question "What?" They describe the situation that the "who" is in. What is going on? What is the "who" dealing with?

Major Arcana

These answer the question "Why?" They describe the lesson you need to learn in this situation and the archetypal energies that need to be expressed. They tell you "why" is the "who" in the "what." The major arcana can also be seen as principles, laws, and psychospiritual needs.

Aces

While aces could be included with the number cards, they tend to express their own particular function. They answer the question, "Where?" They show the elemental world, realm, or sphere where the situation is affecting you most. The significance of the aces was described evocatively by the nineteenth-century French magus, Eliphas Lévi: "The ace of deniers [coins] ... is the soul of the world; the ace of swords is militant intelligence; the ace of cups is loving intelligence; the ace of clubs [wands] is creative intelligence; they are further the principle of motion, progress, fecundity, and power."[2]

The Four Modes Spread

Divide your Tarot deck into four groups:

1. The sixteen court cards

2. The thirty-six number cards

3. The twenty-two major arcana cards

4. The four aces

Shuffle each stack facedown, and pick one card, at random, from each and lay them out in a row. Now interpret the cards in two different ways, as described in the two sections that follow.

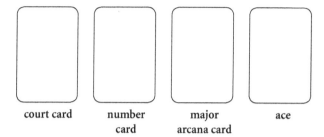

| court card | number card | major arcana card | ace |

What Am I Experiencing?

- The court card is the who. It tells you who you are acting like. Describe the type of person you see in that card.

- The minor arcana number card is the "what." It tells you the situation the "who" is in. Describe the situation and what the "who" is doing in this situation. Use action verbs, if possible.

- The major arcana card is the "why." It tells you why the "who" needs the "what." Describe what archetypal energies within yourself need to be expressed.

- The ace is the "where." It tells you in what elemental realm of consciousness all this is taking place. Describe the sphere or realm or level of consciousness where the "who" is affected by the "why."

How Can I Best Deal with This Situation?

Now, for advice on how to handle the situation, look at the same cards in a different order and from a different perspective. This allows you to see the cards in a fresh way. It also encourages you to use a more empowering perspective, turning a situation that seems to be affecting you, into one that you have chosen in order to learn a lesson or to gain important skills.

Finish the following sentence, and name the cards as you come to them.

- "In the realm shown by (the ace), where . . . (describe this realm),

- "I can use the attributes of (the major arcana card) to . . . (describe the best qualities you see in this card),

- "in order to deal with (the number card), which expresses my desire for/to . . . (describe the situation you have drawn to yourself),

- "as experienced by the court card, the one who . . . (describe that aspect of yourself which chose to experience the situation)."

For Further Work

Three of the four cards in this spread will have suit and elemental designations. See chapter 6 for a discussion of elemental dignities as they can add further insights to your interpretation of this spread.

ENDNOTES

1   The Italian term for the "female pages" in this deck is *fantine*, signifying a female servant.

2   Eliphas Lévi, *Transcendental Magic*, p. 393.

CHAPTER THREE

𝕿he Court in Society

T he court cards, unlike the major arcana of the tarot (which were invented independently), share a common early history with the face
cards found in an ordinary deck of playing cards. The twenty-two major arcana of the tarot appeared at least fifty years after the earliest reports of playing cards in Europe. To understand the original significance of the court
cards, it is thus helpful to look at how playing cards developed and found
their way to fifteenth-century Italy to become part of the tarot deck.

Playing cards, despite the European motif of most decks in use today, are
of Asian origin. Western playing cards probably descended from Chinese
cards that migrated with the Mongol conquerors through Persia to eventually reach western Europe in the fourteenth century. One possible source is
"domino cards," like those the Emperor Mu-tsung and his wife are recorded
using in 969 CE. Chinese dominos corresponded to the fall of two dice of
which there are twenty-one possibilities (the fall of three dice yields fifty-six
possible throws). The Chinese also developed "money cards" in four suits:
coins, strings of coins, myriads of strings of coins, and tens of myriads of
strings of coins. These decks sometimes included three special cards called
"Old Thousand," "Red Flower," and "White Flower," some of which depicted
famous people. Red Flower cards often showed a male with the Chinese character *wang* that, in addition to being a family name, means "king."

In the eleventh century, a nomad tribe called the Seljuks, from the present-day Kazakhstan, conquered Persia and part of both Asia Minor and northern Africa. By the thirteenth century, the great Mongol leaders Genghis Khan and his grandnephew Kublai Khan extended this empire to China. It was through this linking of China and Persia that playing cards probably first came to Persia, appearing between the thirteenth and fourteenth centuries, and may have spread likewise to India. The link is apparent in a card game that was played in India as *Ganjifa*, in Persia as *Ganjifeh*, and in Arabic countries and Egypt as *Kanjifah*.

Mongol rulers, fearful of uprisings, developed a clan of warrior slaves who were taken as children primarily from Christian Turks. They were converted to Islam and sent to the North African coast. They were called *Mamlûks*, meaning "subdued people." By 1250, the Mamlûks had overthrown Saladin's Mongol/Ayyubid dynasty in Egypt and ruled until 1517.

By 1400, the Mamlûks had a card deck consisting of fifty-two cards with suits of swords, polo-sticks, cups, and coins, numbered one through ten, plus three court cards: *malik* ("king"), *na'ib* ("viceroy or deputy"), and *thani na'ib* ("second deputy" or "under-deputy," which was not an actual office in the Islamic dominions of the time). It is this term *na'ib* that apparently came to refer to playing cards in general, for this was the earliest term used for cards in Spain (*naipes*) and Italy (*naibbe* or *naibi*). We may surmise that playing cards were thought of as a "Game of Deputies." The Mamlûks probably brought these cards with them from Persia. They likely entered Christian Europe by way of Spain through the rich culture of the Moors who ruled much of the peninsula until 1492. It is from Catalonia that we have the earliest European records of playing cards and cardmakers. The word *naip* ("playing card") appears in a Catalan rhyming dictionary in 1371. During the years 1377 to 1379, references to playing cards suddenly appear in the records of many cities in western Europe, where they are often described as "newly arrived" or a "new game."

Europeans soon adapted the designs of the Mamlûk cards to reflect their own culture. The Persian suit of *jawkân* or polo sticks was unfamiliar to Europeans as they did not play polo, the game Persians knew as the "sport of kings." In Italy, the shape and aristocratic intent was retained but they were now called *bastoni* (probably meaning a ceremonial baton of office). In Spain they were demoted to *bastos* or cudgels, possibly an adaptation that was a further step removed from the original idea.

SUIT NAMES

China	Persia / Mamlûk	Italy	Spain
wen (coins)	*darâhim* (coins)	*denari* (coins)	*oros* (coins)
suo (strings)	*jawkân* (polo sticks)	*bastoni* (batons)	*bastos* (cudgels)
wan (myriads of strings)	*tûmân* (gold pieces)	*coppe* (cups)	*copas* (cups)
shi (tens of myriads cross-shaped)	*sujûf* (swords)	*spade* (swords)	*espadas* (swords)

The Persian and Mamlûk court cards did not depict images of people, as this was against the laws of Islam, but instead they showed elaborate decorative patterns with the court card titles written on them. In Christian Europe, these were replaced with pictorial images of male figures from three familiar ranks of feudal military hierarchy: a seated and crowned king, a mounted knight, and a standing foot soldier (*fante* in Italian) or servant (French *valet*). These are the court cards still found in Spanish and Italian playing cards today.

By the early 1400s, French, German, and Italian cardmakers were experimenting with variations in both the suits and the court card ranks. Queens sometimes appear, replacing the knight or sometimes the king. Our familiar modern playing cards, with a court of king, queen, and jack, are descended from a fifteenth-century French innovation of this sort.

Although it is uncertain what the number cards (ace through ten) of each suit might have symbolized to the users of the cards in the Islamic and Christian cultures of the time, it seems apparent that the underlying concept of the courts was that of political or social rank, with the king as the highest-ranked figure, and a hierarchy of underlings selected according the social system in place where the cards were made and used.

It is around this time that Tarot decks, with their additional symbolic trump cards, began appearing in northern Italy. Among the hand-painted decks of the nobility, the number and sex of the court cards vary with up to six court cards per suit and an equal number of male and female figures. Despite such variations, most early Tarot decks have a court of four ranks: king, queen, knight, and foot soldier. Although queens are now a familiar feature of modern playing cards and knights seem unusual, it should be remembered that in fifteenth-century Italy where the first Tarot cards appeared, it is the queen who would have been seen as the "extra" rank added to the familiar all-male court.

No records survive to tell us exactly where, when, by whom, or why the first triumph cards—what are now the Tarot—were made. However, the oldest surviving cards known today were made for the ruling family of Milan. The new game and the ornate, hand-painted, gold-leaf-decorated cards used to play it, were originally called *trionfi* ("triumphs" or "trumps"), but by 1516 had become known as *tarocchi*—a name that is still used in Italy today.

Tarot may have arisen out of cosmological and allegorical games and art-of-memory teachings that were part of the emblem tradition of the Renaissance. In such a cosmology, each state or stage triumphs over the previous ones in a kind of hierarchical order, leading from the lowliest figure up to God himself in the World card, depicted as a restored Jerusalem, paradise, or creation as a whole.

It is conceivable that it was the court cards themselves that originally inspired the creation of the Tarot trumps. In the fifteenth-century series of Tarot-like engravings, known as the *Tarocchi del Mantegna*, ten of the fifty designs depict the ranks of European society: beggar, servant, artisan, merchant, gentleman, knight, duke, king, emperor, and finally pope. This series is a sort of systematic merging together of the court card ranks and the lower trumps, with the female figures of queen, empress, and papess excluded from the hierarchy. (The beggar image is reminiscent of the Tarot Fool, and the artisan bears a strong resemblance to the *Bagatto*, or Magician, in early decks.) The higher cards of the Mantegna series sometimes also have parallels in the Tarot trumps: the virtues of Fortitude (Strength), Temperance, and Justice are there, as are the Sun, Moon, and Stars, and the highest cards, Prime Mover and First Cause, may correspond to the World card of the Tarot.

We might imagine a creative person or group of people in early fifteenth-century Italy taking interest in the microcosm of society's hierarchy depicted in the court cards of this newly fashionable recreation of naibi, and thinking how much richer the deck would be if it included powers greater than the kings: the emperor and the pope among human figures, and above them the great forces of the universe: love, death, the devil, the Christian virtues, the sun and moon, and ultimately God himself. Such allegorical hierarchies were already very familiar and popular at the time. Petrarch's fourteenth-century poem *I Trionfi* ("The Triumphs") describes successive victories of love, chastity, death, fame, time, and eternity, and was a mainstay of the popular culture. In addition, the Book of Revelation describes a sequence that parallels the second half of the trump cards.

In our modern, egalitarian age, we are more inclined to see the various cards of the Tarot as equally important and profound. Renaissance Italy, though, was a socially stratified culture of systematic hierarchies and philosophies that emphasized levels of progression from low to high, from human to divine, from mundane to heavenly. If the early creators and users of these cards saw the court as a succinct summary of society and its ranks, they might very well have seen the triumph cards as an elaborate expansion of this concept, extended to include the cosmic powers as well as the earthly ones.

Although we have no direct evidence to know what was on the minds of the designers of the earliest Tarot decks, we may find a new appreciation of the relationship between the court cards and the major arcana by thinking along the aforementioned lines. And although we no longer live in a feudal world, our society still presents us with a set of roles in which we function: parent, artist, laborer, educator, manager, scientist, religious leader, technician, and, of course, hundreds more. These roles, and the individuals who assume them, are important elements in the stories of our lives, and the court cards of the Tarot can help us understand them more clearly.

Historical Personages in Playing Cards

We are accustomed to seeing the figures in a deck of playing cards as nameless icons of their suit and rank. However, there is a long tradition in Europe of associating each of these cards with a person from history or legend.

In 1460, Count Matteo Maria Boiardo (1441–1494) described an unusual deck of trionfi cards in a set of verses—two sonnets and seventy-eight *terzini* ("triplets"), one for each of the tarocchi cards (this work was first published in an anthology in 1523). The four suits were love (darts), hope (vases), jealousy (eyes), and fear (whips). The pip cards in the "good" suits (love and hope) rank from ten down to ace and the "bad" pips (fear and jealousy) ran the other direction "because more love and more hope are better than less, and less jealousy and fear are better than more." The suit associations used here are love (darts) for cups, hope (vases) for pentacles/coins, jealousy (eyes) for wands, fear (whips) for swords. In typical versions of the game of Tarot, coins and cups are ranked with aces highest and tens lowest.

In the late fifteenth century, a tradition arose in France of associating the court cards with historical personages from classical and medieval times, such as Alexander the Great and Charlemagne. These names can still be found today printed on playing card decks used in certain localities in France and Italy. The chart below shows the Boiardo associations, and the titles and a set of interpretations printed on playing cards in England in 1750, taken from W. Gurney Benham, *Playing Cards: Their History and Secrets*. Note that the cards in brackets do not appear in standard playing-card decks.

COURT CARD PERSONAGES

	Boiardo (1460)	French (late 15th century)	English (1750)
Knave of Wands	Hundred-eyed Argus	Lancelot. Later, Arthur or Judas Maccabee, who led the Jewish rebellion against the Syrians).	"Contradiction"
Knave of Cups	Polyphemus (because he loved Galatea)	"La Hire" (Etienne de Vignoles, a mercenary and supporter of Joan of Arc). Later, Paris of Troy or Cyprian (a Roman follower of Aphrodite).	"The sly knave"
Knave of Swords	Phineus	Hogier, the Dane (one of Charlemagne's twelve paladins; patron of hunting who owned two famous swords) or Renaut (also a paladin of Charlemagne).	"The mishievous knave"

	Boiardo (1460)	French (late 15th century)	English (1750)

	Boiardo (1460)	French (late 15th century)	English (1750)
Knave of Coins	Horatius Cocles (noted for his bravery)	Roland / Orlando (hero of the Song of Roland). Later, Hector (who embodied prowess and was slain by Achilles at Troy).	"Jack Shepherd"
[Knight of Wands]	Turnus (rival of Aeneas for the hand of Lavinia)		
[Knight of Cups]	Paris (lover of Helen of Troy)		
[Knight of Swords]	Ptolemy (name of 14 rulers of Egypt)		
[Knight of Coins]	Jason (as he overcame all odds to gain the Golden Fleece)		
Queen of Wands	Juno (Roman goddess whose peacock insignia denoted beauty and jelousy	Floripes; La belle Lucresse (perhaps Lucresse Borgia). Later, Argine, an anagram of "Regina," for Queen Elizabeth I.	"The charming bewitcher"
Queen of Cups	Venus (in a car drawn by swans)	Judith (daughter-in-law of Charlemagne) or Judith who beheaded Holofernes. Later, La belle Heleine (Helen of Troy).	"Beautiful thief"
Queen of Swords	Andromeda (chained to a rock, to be devoured by a sea serpect until rescued by Perseus)	Pallas (Athena). Later, La Pucelle (Joan of Arc).	"Broken heart"
Queen of Coins	Judith of Bethulia (slew Holofernes)	Pentesilea (Queen of the Amazons). Later, Venus, Medea, or Rachel (wife of Jacob).	"The lover's treasure"
King of Wands	Vulcan (because of his jealousy over Mars and Venus)	Alexander the Great (who had hair like a lion's mane). Later, Clovis or Arthur.	"Sir Oliver Rant"
King of Cups	Jupiter (because of his amorous conquests)	Charles (Charlamagne, Holy Roman emperor).	
King of Swords	Dionysius	David (with harp. He cut off Goliath's head with a sword).	"Cupid's useless darts"
King of Coins	Aeneas (because of the hope he sustained traveling from Troy to Italy)	Alexander. Later, and more often, Caesar or Julius Caesar.	"The true lover"

A Journey Through the World of the Tarot Court

This exercise is a meditation to make the court cards come alive in a social and geographical context.

Especially in early decks, the four suits may be thought of as heraldic emblems of four kingdoms, each with its own royal household, depicted in the court cards. We might extend the image further and imagine the "Tarot world" comprising of these four kingdoms, all under the dominion of a common imperial (emperor/empress) and ecclesiastical (pope/papess) authority. Perhaps there is an imperial metropolis as the center of the world, with the four kingdoms extending off in each of the four directions. Look at the imagery of the court cards in your deck and see if you can imagine the geography of the world. (If the deck doesn't show much in the way of landscape, just imagine a place in which the court card figures would appear at home.) Is the kingdom of cups a coastal land? The kingdom of wands a sweltering desert? Perhaps an imaginary world like that of J. R. R. Tolkein's *Lord of the Rings* will suggest four domains to you. In more modern decks, the image of a kingdom may not fit, but other geographical associations can be used—tribes, for example, or neighborhoods, or villages. If your imagination so moves you, you might want to sketch a map of the Tarot world as you envision it.

Take out the court cards of one of the suits, perhaps the one whose imagery projects the strongest sense of place. For each card, ask yourself the following:

- Where is this person likely to be found?
- What role does this person play in the community?
- What responsibilities does this person have?
- What does this person do for recreation?
- How is this person regarded by the local population?

To prepare for the meditation, think of something you would like to know or possess, preferably an abstract quality like "peace of mind" or "financial acumen." Now think of an artifact, a concrete object to symbolize that quality, an object that would fit in with the cultural atmosphere of your deck. (With a traditional medieval-themed deck, for example, financial acumen might be an ornate treasure chest.)

Now sit comfortably, close your eyes, and breathe deeply until you feel re-laxed and centered. Visualize yourself entering the Tarot world, in the do-main of the suit you have selected. Become aware of the details of place: the temperature, the light, the vegetation or buildings, the inhabitants. What is the weather like? What time of year is it? You are here to seek your artifact. Walk around the place, conscious of your quest, but unhurried and open to exploration.

As you travel, allow yourself to encounter the court card personages, one by one. Some you may have to seek out in their own customary places, while others may come to you. If you feel comfortable, make your quest known to them and ask for guidance. Allow the story to unfold naturally.

After your encounter with the last court card personage, bring your explo-ration to an end (or at least a comfortable pausing place), and open your eyes. Record any memorable incidents or conversations. The following questions may be helpful in reflecting on the meditation:

- Which court cards were especially helpful?
- Which were difficult or obstructive?
- Which would you most like to visit again?
- Did you find your artifact? Why or why not?

The Court Progression

As mentioned earlier, the origins of the Tarot court card system are rooted in medieval feudalism. The early Egyptian Mamlûk playing cards had ranks of king, deputy, and second deputy. The Europeans preserved the concept of rank, but drew on the familiar feudal/military model to give a court of king, knight, and foot soldier. In the Tarot deck, this court was expanded to include a queen ranking between the king and knight. In the game of Tarot, this power hierarchy is the essential concept behind the court cards: a king defeats a queen, a queen defeats a knight, and a knight defeats a foot soldier.

Although we no longer live in a feudal society, such power rankings are still very much with us: in the military services, most obviously, but also in many workplaces, and—to varying degrees—in our family structures. And regardless of the other associations Tarot tradition has built upon the court cards, the very words "king" and "queen" (in decks that use those titles) inevitably bring issues of power and authority to mind. The Tarot court cards are thus a valuable window on to power asymmetries in human relationships. We are subject to the control of authority figures, and we also exercise authority over others. The Queen of Swords may be your supervisor at work. At home, you may act as the King of Cups in the eyes of your children or partner.

Some decks move away from the feudal hierarchy implicit in the traditional Tarot. Still, there is usually a ranking present, although it may be subtle. If you lay the court cards from one suit in front of you, it is usually not too difficult to get a picture of who answers to whom. Some decks have moved away from the sexism of the traditional model, ranking queens above kings in some or all of the suits.

In a reading in which several court cards appear, it is often helpful to be sensitive to power issues that may be reflected in the ranks of the cards. Is the page subservient to the king? Are those two knights vying for power in some ritualized combat, like the tournaments of old? Are the king and queen dealing with authority and gender issues in their relationship? When the page or princess is clearly a child or very young person, the cards may relate to feelings of dependency or powerlessness.

Take a fresh look at the significator you chose to represent yourself in the introduction to this book. Where does this card fall in terms of rank? Compare your significator with the other court cards from the same suit. Do you relate to these others as master, servant, or equal? Are these relationships benevolent (perhaps you look up to the kindly king as mentor and guide) or uncomfortable (the overbearing king will not allow you enough freedom to pursue your own goals)? Do the power issues associated with your significator card seem prominent and conspicuous, or are they subtle and secondary? Ask the same questions about your nemesis card. Your responses will depend on the design of the deck you use, as well as your personal reaction to the card. You may want to record some of your observations in your notebook or journal.

Although the power hierarchy may be the most overt progression seen in the Tarot court, at least in terms of its historical origins, there are other interesting progressions to be found there as well. There is often a progression of age or maturity, with the page or princess as the youngest member of the court, and the king (or maybe queen) as the oldest. The page, knight, queen, and king may represent the stages of childhood, adolescence, parenthood or middle age, and elderhood.

Maturity and authority often go hand in hand with a developmental attribute, culminating in wisdom or mastery. From this perspective, the page is a student, the knight is proving his skill by energetically facing his first real-world challenges, the queen has achieved mastery and confidence, and the king has achieved sufficient respect and stature to assume a persona of public command. Alternatively, the queen and king can be seen as having achieved equal levels of mastery, but having different styles, the king's mastery being more task-oriented, and the queen's more relationship-oriented.

Many people see themselves as locked into just a few particular power/authority slots. We have a certain niche at work, with family, and perhaps in a social group, but may not see the nuances of personal authority in different situations. (How do we relate with the clerk at the supermarket, with our child's schoolteacher, or with our friends' children?) But mastery is something we can easily see as situational. One may be a novice golfer but an expert gardener, or an emotionally wise Queen of Cups but an intellectually rough-around-the-edges Knight of Swords. Seeing the court cards as a progression of mastery rather than power is a broader, more versatile way of using the concept of rank in modern life. Still, there are times when simple power is the issue, so it is important to keep that system of meaning in one's reading repertoire.

Of course, one may prefer to move away from the concept of rank entirely, and see the four court cards as four different but equal poles of personality. We'll be exploring this possibility more deeply in the next chapter, where we will look at the court cards in more internal, psychological terms.

The psychological and social terrains interpenetrate a great deal, however. Society assigns a certain stature to the various professions, roles, and activities we take on, and those assignments of stature are transferred, not always consciously, to the different facets of personality appropriate to each of those roles. So we may see the Page of Wands embodying curiosity, for example. But the page's youthfulness and lack of regalia may be a subtle reminder that society seldom sees curiosity as a mark of authority and responsibility, but finds it more appropriate for children, hobbyists, and beginners.

The exercises that follow will help you make a connection between the court cards in your own deck and the social and professional roles that permeate our lives as human beings living in society. Once these connections are established, they can be drawn upon as a useful resource in readings. Although this book emphasizes the psychological perspective on the court cards, it is helpful to have some more concrete associations at one's disposal.

Roles and Professions Exercise

Separate the sixteen court cards from the rest of the deck and randomize their order. Using a sheet of paper, look at each card in turn and write down how well suited the person on the card would be to performing the following roles (you may add roles, or make substitutes, if you think of others you find more interesting):

- parent
- mentor
- philosopher
- assistant
- socialite
- lover
- rival
- organizer
- leader
- artist / poet
- child
- student
- provider
- colleague
- advisor
- friend

Four-Step System to Rate Cards

Use this four-step system to rate the cards in each role:

Mark	Meaning
++	ideal in the role
+	good in the role
-	poor in the role
- -	completely wrong in the role

Consider both the person's competence and maturity and also their comfort level in each role. Avoid stereotypes. Some six-year-olds are not good in the role of child, and some sixty-year-olds are! Don't bog down in considering all the possibilities, but feel free to be a bit thoughtful. You might want to use your imagination and picture the person on the card actually performing the role, perhaps with respect to yourself. Could you imagine approaching the King of Wands as your father, for example?

FOR ADDITIONAL INSIGHTS

Examine your list for patterns by rank and suit. What roles are most or all of the members of a given rank or suit good at? Bad at? Were there any surprises?

Using your work with the roles as a guide, identify three professions at which you think the figure on the court would be successful. You can use this item to bridge the past and present by including both the ancient and modern professions in your consideration, or you can stick with professions appropriate to the time period and cultural context of your deck. While the roles are timeless and general, professions give the card a concrete dimension. This can add clarity and specificity to your readings. For example, you might ask a querent "Was a police officer involved in this situation?" and perhaps trigger a more relevant association than if you say, "This may represent someone with an interest in imposing order and authority."

Career Destiny Spread

This spread uses the court cards to represent professions and career choices. To begin, separate the court cards from the rest of the deck. The querent looks through the court cards faceup and picks out a card to represent each career option being considered. (Sample careers for each court card are given in chapter 9 or use responses to the previous exercise.) There may be two, three, or more cards, depending on how many possibilities the querent is considering. Arrange these court cards side by side, in whatever order seems most appropriate. These are the cards in position 4, shown as "Career A," "Career B," etc., in the spread diagram on the next page. Return the remaining court cards to the deck, shuffle, and deal out the other cards in the spread, working from the bottom up, starting with "Underlying Question" and ending with "Destiny." The number of cards dealt will depend on how many career options the querent has identified. Each career option will have its own assets, challenges, and outcome. The diagram shows how the spread appears for two career options, A and B.

CAREER DESTINY SPREAD

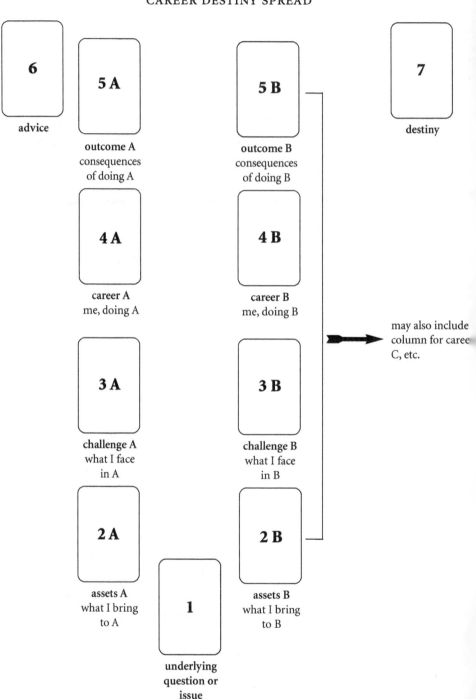

6

advice

5 A

outcome A
consequences
of doing A

5 B

outcome B
consequences
of doing B

7

destiny

4 A

career A
me, doing A

4 B

career B
me, doing B

may also include
column for caree[r]
C, etc.

3 A

challenge A
what I face
in A

3 B

challenge B
what I face
in B

2 A

assets A
what I bring
to A

1

2 B

assets B
what I bring
to B

underlying
question or
issue

UNDERLYING QUESTION OR ISSUE

1. The career choice may stem from some deeper question with which the querent is dealing, which may not be acknowledged. This card gives a glimpse of the issues motivating the querent's need to choose between different career paths at this time. Pay close attention to this card; it may suggest an approach that has nothing to do with a new career at all.

2. Assets—These cards show what resources the querent brings to each possible career path. These may be talents, relationships, material resources, or relevant experience and history.

3. Challenges—These cards show the obstacles the querent can expect to encounter in pursuing each of the paths. They may be difficult situations, temptations, or interference from other aspects of the querent's life.

4. Careers—These are the court cards that the querent originally selected to represent the different career options. In a way, they are like multiple "significators" showing the persona the querent takes on in each of the possible careers. Even though the querent has chosen these cards ahead of time, they should be looked at carefully when interpreting the spread, in terms of how they relate to each other and to the other cards that appear.

5. Outcomes—These cards show a likely outcome resulting from pursuing each career path. These may be immediate consequences or long-term results. Remember that a decision as large as a career choice will have a great many different effects on the querent's life. The card shows only one of them.

6. Advice—Although the outcome cards may suggest which path is most beneficial, their role is more to provide snapshots of what lies ahead on each path. The advice card actually offers a suggestion about how the decision should be made. It may sometimes suggest

which path to choose, but more often will comment on how to make the choice and what factors to take into account.

7. Destiny—This card shows where the querent may ultimately be headed. It often looks past the immediate career choice into a more distant condition or challenge. The destiny card should be compared with the outcome cards to give insight about which choice will help the querent achieve (or avoid) what appears in the destiny card.

Because this spread uses court cards to signify the career options, court cards that come up in other positions may have a special significance. Unless they clearly show people in the querent's life or relevant facets of the querent's personality, they should be seen as other careers beyond those the querent included among the possible options. A court card appearing in one of the asset positions, for example, might represent an earlier career that helps pave the way for the new one. A court card in an outcome position may indicate that if the querent follows that path, he or she may end up in a career different from the one actually chosen. The future is larger than our plans. Reta Beebe, a scientist who worked on the Voyager space missions to Jupiter and the outer planets, often told her students, "When I was in college, my profession didn't exist yet."

Especially when reading for others, it is important to emphasize that no major life decision should be made on the basis of one source of information alone. A Tarot reading, as helpful as it can be in clarifying issues and suggesting a course of action, offers only one perspective on a decision.

Storytelling Spread

The seventy-eight cards of the Tarot are symbolic building blocks composing the stories of our lives. After you get to know the meaning of each card, the Tarot becomes a sort of shorthand language for describing the experiences of life. It's a fun and useful exercise to watch a movie or read a novel, and see if you can summarize the plot, characters, and themes of the story using Tarot cards. The idea is that by teaching yourself to "speak Tarot," you become fluent and can more easily appreciate the message the cards have for you in a reading.

Let's take this a step further and see if spreading the cards can inspire us to imagine a fictional story, complete with plot, characters, and themes. If you enjoy creative writing, you might want to actually write out a short story, film script, or play based on working with this spread. If not, you can still construct a tale in your imagination. This activity can be lots of fun, as it lets you practice interpreting the cards without the pressure of relating them to a real-life situation.

Shuffle the deck however you please. To write your story, you will arrange the cards into three rows as follows: the top row is reserved for the major arcana, the middle row for the number cards (ace through ten of each suit), and the bottom row for the court cards. In storytelling terms, the top row is for themes, the middle row for plot events, and the lower row for characters. Draw from the top of the deck, place the cards from left to right within their appropriate rows. The first card in each row is placed at the far left, lined up with the first card in the other two rows. One of the rows (often the middle row) may grow faster than the others. When you draw a card that belongs in one of the shorter rows, place it above or below the rightmost card in the longest row, even though that will leave some gaps. This is a way of keeping the three rows synchronized, nearly the same length, even though some will have fewer cards. Continue drawing and placing cards until you have drawn at least six cards, and have at least one card in each row, with a minimum of two cards in the court card (character) row.

Example

I draw the Ten of Swords and lay it down. Next comes the Eight of Swords, which I place to the right of the Ten. The third card is the Two of Cups, which goes to the right of the Eight of Swords. Next is the Page of Cups, the first "character" (court) card, so it is the first card in the bottom row, placed directly below the Ten of Swords. Next comes the King of Wands, another character card. To keep the rows even, it is placed directly below the Two of Cups, leaving a gap between the page and king. Next comes the Nine of Cups, placed just right of the Two of Cups. Finally, I draw the Emperor, which is the first "theme" (major arcana) card, and so it is placed directly above the Ten of Swords. At this point, I have at least one card in each row and at least six cards total (there are actually seven), so the spread is complete. It looks like this:

Storytelling spread with cards from The Robin Wood Tarot

Themes: Emperor

Plot: Ten of Swords   Eight of Swords   Two of Cups   Nine of Cups

Characters: Page of Cups   King of Wands

To find the story in the cards, begin by focusing on the themes. In this example, there is only one theme: the Emperor. It might be a story about power and authority, a story about fatherhood, or the laws and rules of society. Bring to mind the different concepts you associate with the Emperor, and focus on one of them as an underlying idea or basic premise or lesson of the story.

Next, look at the character cards. The first one is the Page of Cups, so this will be the focal character as the story begins. Draw on your understanding of this card to establish the basic personality of this character. Then go further, and look at the card to answer questions about this character: age, physical appearance, profession, interests, etc.

The second character, the King of Wands, has not been "introduced" yet, but makes an appearance later in the story line, so we'll leave him aside for the moment and turn our attention to the plot line.

The first event is the Ten of Swords, perhaps a disaster or defeat of some kind, even a death. Imagine the character you saw in the Page of Cups card participating in this event. Is he or she the victim, a witness, or perhaps the perpetrator, even? Put the event in concrete terms for your story. It is unlikely to be a person literally speared by ten swords, as in the card image. Perhaps it is an event that ruins a promising career, the breakup of a relationship, or the death of a loved one. Settle on a concrete image of what has happened.

The second plot event is the Eight of Swords. Perhaps the defeat experienced in the ten has left our page character feeling trapped, helpless, unable to move forward and begin a new life. If the Ten of Swords was the loss of a career, the Eight might be a series of episodes in which our character's hopes for new employment are blocked off, and the character can't see why that is happening or find a way out.

As you continue to develop the plot in this way, refer frequently back to the theme. In this case, the theme card is the Emperor. Perhaps it is a powerful institution, like a political party or a corporate monopoly, that our focus character is up against.

Next, the King of Wands makes an entrance, in a scene represented by the Two of Cups. It could be a romantic encounter or a sudden friendship and alliance. Establish the King of Wands character by interpreting the card and answering questions, just as was done for the Page of Cups.

The story's final scene is represented by the Nine of Cups. Perhaps our page's wishes and desires are finally achieved, after the King of Wands has helped remove the blindfold and barriers. The ending should be carefully thought through, so as to reconnect with the theme. Perhaps it offers a thoughtful lesson on how to succeed in the face of opposition from institutions of power.

Putting together a story from a handful of Tarot cards in this way not only exercises one's interpretive imagination, but also reinforces the different roles that major arcana, number cards, and court cards often play in a reading. Beginners often try to read every Tarot card as an event that will come about in the querent's future. With this approach, court cards can be very confusing, as they frequently do not depict happenings, but rather individual personalities in rather static poses. But no great play, movie, or novel was ever made just by stringing events together. Interesting characters and themes are equally important. The meaning of a court card in a reading is often not about what will happen, but rather who will be involved. Similarly, the major arcana may direct us toward the "why" behind events.

Sample Movie Synopsis: The Page of Cups

Let's have fun with this spread, and make a concrete story out of it, a film script, say. The exercise is especially entertaining if you use visual details from each card in a concrete, literal way. Lay out the cards from the example given above. *The Robin Wood Tarot* deck was used but you might find it interesting to compare the results using a different deck. Try to identify each scene, to be explained in the following paragraphs, with a corresponding card.

The theme of this movie is about what it takes to be a "man." The first court card is the Page of Cups and he represents an artistic, overly sensitive, and imaginative adolescent twelve-year-old boy. His father views him with disgust and despairs that he will never grow up to be anything but a sissy—therefore he stresses the tough-guy style when around his son. After an especially nasty argument (or "battle") over a meal, the boy (Jordan) goes out fishing. He witnesses a murder and is discovered. A terrifying hunt ensues, and the boy is captured by the murderer who leaves him tied and blindfolded in an abandoned boat house to die slowly.

The father, the King of Wands, is having an affair, and uses the boathouse to meet with his lover. He is a widower, but every time he goes out with a woman, Jordan has a severe asthma attack—almost dying on more than one occasion—and so the father is forced to conduct his relationship in secret. While lying in the boathouse loft, Jordan overhears his father talk about his love for his son and his distress and fear that Jordan will never be able to share in a family with the woman he loves—that is, until the boy "toughens up." He hears them make love, with poetry and beauty, and discovers that his father is capable of tenderness—an attribute the father has never shown to his son. Finally the boy is able to knock something over to make a noise that draws his father's attention. The father almost brains him with an oar before he realizes it is his son. Once freed, the boy tells his father about the murder and they go to the sheriff.

The murderer is identified and caught (he was a serial killer having murdered ten people), and the boy receives a huge reward, which he shares with his father and new stepmother. He has learned how facing death and acknowledging love are the two sides of being a man. The movie ends with a scene at the family dinner table where his stepmother toasts Jordan, saying how lucky she is to be with the two finest "men" in the county.

CHAPTER FOUR

ℭhe Court Within

The single most powerful way of viewing the court cards of the Tarot
is as facets of human personality. Personality is the totality of qualities and character traits—behavioral, temperamental, emotional, and mental—that are peculiar to an individual person. To a large degree, our lives are
personality-driven. Understanding our own propensities, preferences, and
quirks, as well as those of others, is essential to living.

Our language is full of words describing personality. Some of them come
from theoretical models (introverted, sanguine, passive-aggressive), but many
more are just part of the simple vocabulary of daily life: happy-go-lucky,
mean-spirited, hotheaded, shy.

For ages, people have hoped that a single system of categories would un-
lock the secrets of human personality and, once and for all, clue us in, let us
know what to expect when dealing with that most unpredictable of creatures,
the human being. The ultimate personality model has not been found, of
course, but many of the attempted solutions offer fascinating insights and dis-
till some portion of our accumulated wisdom.

Regardless of the details, the essential concept is that the landscape of
human personality can be divided up into a manageable number of distinct
territories.

Astrology

Astrology is perhaps the most elaborate system for analyzing personality, given its twelve signs, seven (or, in modern forms, ten or more) planets, twelve houses, and a plethora of aspects and combinations. The sun sign alone offers twelve distinct personality categories, often characterized by keywords such as these:

- Aries: headstrong, decisive, impulsive, showing initiative, independent, self-aware
- Taurus: protective, stubborn, loyal, resourceful, productive, stable
- Gemini: loquacious, two-sided, outgoing, rational, intelligent, skillful, communicative
- Cancer: domestic, nurturing, private, protective, sensitive, secure
- Leo: dramatic, optimistic, fun-loving, proud, creative, demonstrative
- Virgo: organized, practical, industrious, discriminating, critical, analytical, efficient
- Libra: indecisive, harmony-seeking, flirtatious, balancing, diplomatic
- Scorpio: intense, secretive, moody, transformative, regenerating
- Sagittarius: adventurous, inquisitive, philosophical, expansive, searching for meaning
- Capricorn: competent, status-conscious, acquisitive, accomplished, structured, organized
- Aquarius: philanthropic, idealistic, creative, original, rebellious, agent of change
- Pisces: dreamy, sensitive, intuitive, compassionate, sacrificing, idealistic

The astrological signs are often thought to correspond with the court cards. Since there are sixteen cards and only twelve signs, four court cards are left unassigned (usually the pages). Both the suits of the Tarot and the signs of astrology are also connected with the classical elements, as follows:

- Fire (usually wands or swords) is assigned to Aries, Leo, and Sagittarius

- Water (cups) to Cancer, Scorpio, and Pisces
- Air (usually swords or wands) to Libra, Aquarius, and Gemini
- Earth (pentacles) to Capricorn, Taurus, and Virgo

Within each elemental group, the actual assignment of signs to court card ranks differs from deck to deck.

Myers-Briggs Type Indicator (MBTI)

More modern systems of categorizing personality are based not on the positions of the sun, moon, and planets at one's birth, but instead on observed or reported personality tendencies. Katherine Briggs and Isabel Briggs Myers devised a personality typing system based on the Jungian psychology. The Myers-Briggs system places each person on one side or the other of four personality axes:

- Extroverted / Introverted (E/I): Extroverts draw energy from interacting with others, think out loud, and prefer action to study. Introverts draw energy from solitude, think carefully before speaking, and are more interested in understanding things than changing them.

- Intuitive / Sensing (N/S): Intuitives prefer generalizations to specifics, get bored with details, and think abstractly. Sensing types appreciate concrete details, clear procedures, and practical results.

- Thinking / Feeling (T/F): Thinkers filter out emotion and rely on logic, are concerned with objectivity and impartiality, and see decision making as problem solving. Feelers are concerned with relationships, interpersonal harmony, and make decisions on the basis of emotional and personal consequences.

- Judging / Perceiving (J/P): Judgers like to structure their experiences and keep their lives scheduled and organized. Perceivers take the world as it comes, valuing spontaneity and surprise.

Because there are two possibilities in each of these four personality factors, the Myers-Briggs typing gives 2 x 2 x 2 x 2 = 16 combinations, exactly the same as the number of court cards. Several systems of correspondence between

Myers-Briggs types and court cards have been suggested, but they are not usually made explicit in the design of Tarot decks as the astrological correspondences have been.

Finding exact correspondences between the MBTI and court cards is difficult since the MBTI is not based on age, development, or on gender distinctions. On the other hand, by using the MBTI, we can see each court card as a whole person of any age and sex and as having a specific set of skills, needs, and proclivities. In fact, you can now determine your significator "scientifically" by taking a test such as the Keirsey Temperament Sorter (see bibliography) to find out which type and, therefore, which court card you are. The fact that there is a lack of agreement as to which type goes with which court card means that, if you want to use this system, you should study the materials available and decide what works best for you. Jung's types generally correspond as follows: wands are intuitive (N), cups are feeling (F), swords are thinking (T), and pentacles are sensing (S). This is usually the starting point for any comparison.

The chart that follows shows three systems for combining the MBTI with the court cards. The systems were developed by Mary K. Greer, Jana Riley, and Linda Gail Walters, respectively.[1] The systems used by Greer and Riley are based more strongly on matching MBTI descriptions to card meanings rather than being primarily consistent with a theoretical system. The system proposed by Linda Gail Walters is, in her own words, "both internally and externally consistent, a single unique pair of indicators corresponds to one, and only one, suit / element, and another unique pair of indicators corresponds to one, and only one, card rank." Both Walters and Riley see all pages and queens as introverts (I) while kings and knights are extroverts (E). For Walters, all kings and queens use the judging (J) faculty to make decisions, while all pages and knights use the more open, perceiving faculty (P). Additionally, Walters sees all wands as intuitive-thinking (NT), all cups as intuitive-feeling (NF), all swords as sensing-thinking (ST), and all pentacles as sensing-feeling (SF). Walters has proposed the most elegant system, one that has the advantage of being both logical and the easiest to remember once you understand the basic principles. However, it makes all the "female" cards introverts and all the "male" cards extroverts, a social assumption that is not true in real life and that many people will find limiting. Additionally, many of the MBTI type descriptions seem to fit a different selection of court cards far better.

A more detailed chart with descriptive names for each type can be found in appendix B. Books on the MBTI can be found in the bibliography.

		Wands (N)	Cups (F)	Swords (T)	Pentacles (S)
Kings	Greer	E<u>N</u>TP	ES<u>F</u>P	ES<u>T</u>J	E<u>S</u>TP
	Riley	E<u>N</u>TP	ES<u>F</u>J	ES<u>T</u>J	E<u>S</u>TP
	Walters	E<u>NT</u>J	EN<u>F</u>J	ES<u>T</u>J	E<u>SF</u>J
Queens	Greer	I<u>N</u>TJ	IS<u>F</u>P	IN<u>T</u>P	I<u>ST</u>J
	Riley	I<u>N</u>TJ	IS<u>F</u>P	IS<u>T</u>P	I<u>ST</u>J
	Walters	I<u>NT</u>J	I<u>NF</u>J	I<u>ST</u>J	I<u>SF</u>J
Knights	Greer	E<u>N</u>FP	IN<u>F</u>P	EN<u>T</u>J	E<u>S</u>FJ
	Riley	E<u>N</u>FP	EN<u>F</u>J	EN<u>T</u>J	E<u>S</u>FP
	Walters	E<u>N</u>TP	EN<u>F</u>P	E<u>ST</u>P	E<u>S</u>FP
Pages	Greer	I<u>N</u>FJ	EN<u>F</u>J	IS<u>T</u>P	I<u>S</u>FJ
	Riley	I<u>N</u>FJ	IN<u>F</u>J	IN<u>T</u>P	I<u>S</u>FJ
	Walters	I<u>NT</u>P	IN<u>F</u>P	I<u>ST</u>P	I<u>S</u>FP

* Note: The underlined letters indicate the suit's predominant identifying characteristic.

Cattell's 16PF

All personality typing systems, whether ancient or modern, depend strongly on empirical experience about how personality characteristics tend to cluster into recognizable patterns. A modern system that is based almost exclusively on empirical data, without a preconceived theoretical model behind it, is the 16PF system, devised by Raymond Cattell in 1949. He drew an extensive sample of personality-related words from an unabridged dictionary, and asked subjects to decide whether each word applied to their own personality (or the personality of someone they knew). He found that groups of words often "traveled together"—if one applied to a particular person, so did the others in the group. Most of the information about someone's personality could be captured by how strongly they matched each of sixteen "personality factors"—each standing for a group of correlated personality words. Cattell's sixteen factors are:

1. Warmth

2. Reasoning

3. Emotional stability

4. Dominance

5. Liveliness

6. Rule-consciousness

7. Social boldness

8. Sensitivity

9. Vigilance

10. Abstractedness

11. Privateness

12. Apprehensiveness

13. Openness to change

14. Self-reliance

15. Perfectionism

16. Tension

Some of these words have rather specialized meanings in the context of Cattell's 16PF system. The factors that account for the strongest differences between people are listed first in the list, with less important factors toward the bottom.

Many modern personality tests are based on a similar principle: the person taking the test selects whether a certain personality preference accurately describes him or her, and then the responses are sorted into whatever system of categories the designers of the test are using. The exercise that follows will acquaint you with some of your own personality preferences, and then give you an opportunity to examine court card personalities through the same lens.

Personality Quiz

Here's a personality questionnaire that is not at all scientific, but can still be illuminating and interesting. It uses twelve distinct traits, each with an opposite. The traits are listed below. Following each are a few brief examples to better illustrate each trait. You might want to read these through first, and make sure you have a clear sense of how the traits differ from each other.

- Friendly: makes people feel comfortable, enjoys company
  Opposite: cold

- Intelligent: insightful, analytical
  Opposite: slow

- Calm: patient, also not easily frustrated
  Opposite: short-tempered

- Fun-loving: is the life of the party, jokes around a lot
  Opposite: serious

- Dutiful: tries to follow rules, respects authority
  Opposite: rebellious

- Suspicious: suspects hidden motives, finds it hard to forgive
  Opposite: trusting

- Sensitive: sentimental, easily moved
  Opposite: stoical

- Assertive: takes charge, speaks out
  Opposite: docile

- Imaginative: daydreams, shows creativity
  Opposite: practical

- Reserved: hard to get to know, keeps thoughts to oneself
  Opposite: open

- Anxious: worries a lot, afraid of doing the wrong thing
  Opposite: carefree

- Perfectionist: efficient, demanding on self
  Opposite: casual

After you have read the descriptions and have a sense of what each trait means, determine your own personality with respect to each of the traits. Decide whether you show the trait (mark with a +), show the trait strongly (++), show the opposite of the trait (-), or show the opposite of the trait strongly (--). There's no middle ground between "shows the trait" and "shows the opposite trait" because it's important that you make a definite judgment, even if you might be able to see both possibilities in yourself. Go through the list of traits quickly. Don't sit and stew over each one, just respond with your impulses. If you get stuck on a particular trait, skip it and come back to it after you've gone through the list.

Now repeat the exercise for each of the court cards in your deck. Pick up the sixteen cards and randomize them, so they are in no particular order, and go through them one by one, rating each card on each trait. That may seem like a lot of work, but remember to just go through rapidly and trust your first impressions, and it won't take long.

Now arrange all sixteen court cards from a single deck in a 4 x 4 matrix, so you can see, for example, all the cups in one column going down, and all the kings in one row going across. Look at the four cards in each row (rank) and the four cards in each column (suit) and see if you can identify similarities and differences between the cards in each group of four. For example, are all the knights assertive? Are all the cups sensitive?

In the process of doing this exercise, the personalities of the various court cards should start to crystallize in your mind. As you become aware of key traits that capture the essence of each card, record them in your journal.

Subpersonalities

Every person has the capacity to demonstrate all different facets of personality. No one is limited to a single category.

Perhaps the most expected personality changes occur over time. We grow, discover new approaches, and gradually (or sometimes suddenly) evolve into different people than we were when we were younger. Usually, this process makes us more versatile. A parent with a responsible job might be genuinely dutiful most of the time, but still be able to understand youthful rebellious-ness and display this trait in certain contexts.

Over time, we also learn to hide our natural inclinations, substituting be-haviors that others expect of us. We all have a collection of personality "masks" we wear in different situations. We may be serious and conscientious at work, glib and witty with friends, calm and gentle with loved ones, and then passion-ate and sentimental when writing in a personal diary or journal. This is one of the things that makes personality questionnaires, like the one in the previous section, hard to answer quickly—we can always think of situations in which we behave differently.

Also, there are personality traits that we have learned (or chosen) to dislike. It may be very difficult to acknowledge such traits within ourselves, but that does not mean they are absent. Our self-image may be as much about what we are not, as it is about what we are. In Jungian terms, the personality traits we refuse to acknowledge in ourselves make up our shadow, a kind of mirror image of who we think we are. Refusing to acknowledge our own shadow, we often find ourselves at odds with other people who exhibit those traits as part of their outward personality—they can become symbols of everything we hope to defeat and suppress, or everything that we secretly long for.

The nemesis card you selected at the same time as your significator in the introduction to this book may offer some clues about your shadow self. The nemesis, being the court card most unlike yourself, may encapsulate person-ality traits you'd rather not acknowledge to the world, or even to yourself.

Each court card thus represents some aspect of yourself—perhaps your self-image (the significator), a mask, a former self, a future self, an ideal self, or a shadow self (like the nemesis). Because of this, every court card that ap-pears in a reading has the potential to cast light on the workings of your own personality, even while it may also represent another person. When you iden-tify a court card with someone else, then that person is a teacher, guide, or model for you to better understand how their personality type is also a sub-personality in yourself. You can specifically determine how that personality manifests in you and what it has to offer. A fully integrated personality seeks to understand and accept all parts of him- or herself.

Court Cards in Your Closet

There are many ways to determine the roles you play and the varied aspects of yourself. One that may hold some surprises for you is to go mentally through your closet and look at the clothes you find there. Who are the different characters within you? Who wears these outfits? After you've read the following example, close your eyes, and see your closet in front of you. Look through it. There may be, for example, your business-suited downtown self, your casual weekend persona, and your Saturday night special. Then there's the hiker, biker, skier, swimmer, boater, and runner. And what about those sensual nightclothes, or that outfit stuck in the back that your mother bought you ages ago, or your equally buried hippie, disco, or goth togs waiting for a revival. Are the paint-spattered jeans those of an artist or a house painter? What other personas lie there in wait for you? List the different roles you've found.

Another place to look for your roles is on your bookshelf, with its old and new interests, its hobby and activity guides, and your fantasies of what you'd like to do and be. If you need more, then look in scrapbooks and picture albums. What are you to all the different people in your life—parent, child, lover, friend, boss, employee, co-worker, teacher, student, nature-lover, jock? Obviously there are a lot of "yous" around.

Let's take a look at all these facets of yourself, which are like the facets on a cut crystal, reflecting different aspects under different lights.

Make a list of at least six or seven of the major roles you play or masks you wear in your life right now. Select court cards that most correspond to each role or aspect of yourself. A court card can appear more than once.

After you have chosen your cards, answer the following questions:

- Have you used all the suits?
- If some are missing, which are they and what qualities do they represent?
- Where in your life do you manifest these missing qualities? Add these roles or aspects to your list along with the court card that most corresponds.
- What suit predominates? What does this say about conditions in which you are most comfortable?

- Is there any rank (king, queen, knight, page) that you didn't choose and with which you don't easily identify? Which is it? What developmental level would it be? What qualities does this missing figure(s) represent that you haven't listed among your roles?

- Which rank appears most often? Do you feel this is most characteristic of yourself?

Look at the four kings. Acknowledge some area of your life in which you have developed outer or public mastery and can demonstrate it to others. In this you are kingly. Pick one of the kings to represent this in yourself. State this expertise.

Look at the four queens. Acknowledge some area of your life in which you have developed intra- or interpersonal mastery and can nurture that in yourself or another. In this you are queenly. Pick one of the queens to represent this in yourself. State this expertise.

Look at the four knights. Acknowledge an area of your life in which you are actively using a skill or putting energy into an exploratory or revolutionary action. Where are you on a quest? In this you are knightly. Pick one of the knights to represent this in yourself. State your skill, action or quest.

Look at the four pages (or princesses). Acknowledge an area of your life in which you are being playful, taking a risk, learning something new or acquiring some information through your senses. In this you are like a youthful page. Pick one of the pages to represent this in yourself. State how you are like this.

For instance, as a mother relating to my daughter, I am most like the Queen of Cups. When writing books, I become the Queen of Swords. I am the King of Wands when expounding passionately on my favorite topic—the Tarot. To my own mother I will always be her Page of Cups. In my determination to create a stable financial base I am the Knight of Pentacles.

Jungian Archetypes and Personality Structures

Based on classical theories of the four elements, humors, and temperaments, Carl Jung developed a quaternity of functions or psychological types that he named: intuition, feeling, thinking, and sensation (see discussion of the Myers-Briggs Personality Type Indicator on page 65). We have related these to the suits of wands, cups, swords, and pentacles, respectively. They may likewise be attributed to the four ranks of king, queen, knight, and page. Followers of Jung believed there must be four-part psychic structures that describe aspects of the mature masculine and feminine. These models are applied to the court cards below. If you find the Jungian model useful, then consider using the ideas, without the need for following them slavishly. The key to this model is to realize that the whole person must integrate all four aspects of conscious maturity to form an aware self. Furthermore, the contra-sexual aspects can be seen as aspects of the unconscious—what Jung called the anima if you are a male or animus if you are a female. When we project an archetype onto another we are often left feeling bereft and lacking in those qualities. See the discussion of projection on page 87.

The Mature Feminine

Toni Wolff, Jung's longtime muse and lover, felt Jung lacked an understanding of the feminine self, and in 1956, she identified four "Structural Forms of Relatedness in the Feminine Psyche" (discussed in *Knowing Woman: A Feminine Psychology* by Irene de Castillejo). These correspond with the four queens. Because they focus on women in relationships, they do not express a full range of the feminine quaternities, but still can be helpful in understanding the corresponding queens. When these forms are projected onto others, rather than owned in ourselves, it is like giving away some of our abilities and choices.

QUEEN OF WANDS AS THE HETAIRA ARCHETYPE

The hetaira or companion archetype has very personal, one-on-one relationships with individuals in her life. Children are of secondary importance. She is the *femme inspiratrice*. Like the courtesan, she is accomplished and masterful. In modern times, she seeks her own inspiration, and is most concerned with self-growth and development of individuation.

In her negative (or reversed) manifestation, she becomes the seductress, or she rebels against cultural mores and limitations. When this archetype is projected onto others, we feel out of touch with our inspiration and stuck in stultifying situations.

QUEEN OF CUPS AS THE MEDIAL ARCHETYPE

The medial archetype, or medium, has impersonal relationships with individuals. She is a psychic, wise woman, or priestess. According to de Castellijo, she is permeated by the unconscious of another (or by some form of collective unconscious) and makes that unconscious thought, feeling, or desire visible by living it. She may dream other people's dreams or assist someone in dying. She develops inner perception.

In her negative (or reversed) manifestation, she becomes either the abused victim or angel of perfection and can lose her own ego identity to a person or group, becoming vague and unfocused. When this archetype is projected onto others, we feel out of touch with our inner wisdom and knowing.

QUEEN OF SWORDS AS THE AMAZON ARCHETYPE

The amazon archeytpe has impersonal relationships with groups of people—like being a warrior for a cause. She is independent, self-contained, and daring. Stressing platonic relationships, she is not dependent on anyone else for fulfilment, but appreciates challenges and rivalry that help her hone and refine skills.

In her negative (or reversed) manifestation, she is either the critic or exile and may deny longings for what seems perpetually out of reach. When this archetype is projected onto others, we feel weak and subservient and unable to handle loss.

QUEEN OF PENTACLES AS THE MOTHER ARCHETYPE

The mother archetype has personal relationships with groups of people. This is how we tend to conceive Mother Earth, or those women who nourish all the children in a community. There is a wholehearted support and acceptance of the generative force. She cares for and protects whatever is new and growing.

In her negative (or reversed) manifestation, she becomes the predator who attacks those who threaten her offspring, or she becomes the possessive, smothering mother. When this archetype is projected onto others, we feel insecure, undervalued, useless, and not able to mother the self.

The Mature Masculine

Robert Moore and Douglas Gillette responded to a young man's question "Where are the initiated men of power today?" by writing their book *King, Warrior, Magician, Lover: Rediscovering the Archetypes of the Mature Masculine.* These four archetypes fit the four kings quite well. Reading this book can enrich your experience of both the court cards and several of the major arcana.

Moore and Gillette only identified one of the major arcana with Jung's four functions—the lover with sensation, which would affiliate him with the pentacles suit, however cups and water prove to be more likely—at least as relates to the Tarot. Reading their description of the Lover, however, might change your mind.

KING OF WANDS AS KING ARCHETYPE

The king archetype has two main functions: to give order and to provide fertility and blessing. He is responsible for the well-being of the land and people—if he becomes sick, weak, or impotent, the people languish. The king must appear before his people. A sense of self-worth and value comes from being seen. He brings stability and balance and mediates vitality, life force, and joy. He encourages creativity, and guides and nurtures others toward their own fullness of being. To some extent, he exists in all the kings.

In his negative (or reversed) manifestation, he becomes either the tyrant or the weakling. According to Moore and Gillette, when we project the king energy to some other person, "we experience ourselves as impotent, as incapable of acting, incapable of feeling calm and stable." When this archetype is projected onto a public leader or organization, we may lose our ability to reason and act independently.

KING OF CUPS AS LOVER ARCHETYPE

Although Moore and Gillette relate the lover energy to Jung's sensation function, it has far more cups energy. Its characteristics include vitality, passion, and appetite for life. The lover is deeply sensual and not ashamed of his pleasure or his body. He experiences an intimate contact with everything around him, and feels primal hungers passionately. He wants to touch the world in its totality. He is aesthetically attuned to the environment.

In his negative (or reversed) manifestation, he becomes either the addicted or the impotent lover. As the addict, he becomes possessed and lost, living only for the pleasure in the moment. Moore and Gillette say he is "boundary-less" and overwhelmed by the unconscious as if by the sea (a definite King of Cups quality). The impotent lover is bored, listless, and depressed. When this archetype is projected onto others, we lack passion and joy.

KING OF SWORDS AS WARRIOR ARCHETYPE

The main characteristics of the warrior archetype are aggressiveness, clarity of thinking and alertness, strategy, self-discipline and skill through training, adaptability, and awareness of death. They also include loyalty and devotion to a transpersonal ideal or goal, which makes the warrior inaccessible because of his emotional detachment. He destroys to make way for something new and fresh. The warrior can also be discerned in the four knights.

In his negative (or reversed) manifestation, he becomes either the sadist or the masochist, both involving cruelty. He can also become the workaholic who is out to "save" others through sacrificing his own well-being. When this archetype is projected onto others, we become cowardly and we procrastinate, feeling defeated before we even begin.

KING OF PENTACLES AS MAGICIAN ARCHETYPE

The magician archetype is the user of secret knowledge, the knower and master of technology, and a container and channeler of power. In magic, the pentacle serves a similar function. As a steward of sacred space, he guides processes of transformation and is aware of the secrets of nature, the stars, the weather, and the hunt. Moore and Gillette call it the "observing ego" that monitors and controls the flow of energy or emotions in the self, working to transform raw power to usefulness. It is the archetype of thoughtfulness, reflection, and introversion.

In his negative (or reversed) manifestation, he becomes either the manipulator or the denying "innocent" one. We find this influence in the proliferation of toxic wastes and pollution, or in taking advantage of others through specialized knowledge, which leads to false superiority, isolation, and loneliness. The "innocent one" doesn't know anything, isn't responsible, and is slippery and elusive. When this archetype is projected onto others, we lack security and are vulnerable to outside pressures.

The Child Archetype

Moore and Gillette also discuss "boy psychology," which will be modified here to express immature aspects of both the male and female consciousness— what has come to be known as the "inner child." It is most fully equated with the pages. Knights tend to combine a less mature masculine energy described above in the warrior archetype with the hero aspect of the child. The child archetype suggests playfulness, pleasure, fun, energy, open-mindedness, enthusiasm, adventure, freshness, and newness. Again, all four aspects need to be integrated in the self. When assimilating previously denied parts of the mature self, there may be a temporary and terrifying regression to the child, as one goes through an initiatory experience likened to a mythic dismemberment.

PAGE OF WANDS AS DIVINE CHILD ARCHETYPE

The divine child is God-like and narcissistic, but also open and vulnerable. This archetype is about mystery, miracles, and wonder. It brings light and joy. Creative aspects are bursting into awareness but, being fragile, must be encouraged and protected.

In this child's negative (or reversed) manifestation, he or she becomes either an arrogant tyrant, full of pride (i.e., hubris), or a fatigued and frightened weakling. When this archetype is projected onto others, we are left feeling jaded and pessimistic.

PAGE OF CUPS AS OEDIPAL CHILD (OR EROS) ARCHETYPE

This child is concerned with connectedness, warmth, and affection. Moore and Gillette see this aspect as the child who must learn to relate to the spiritual parent, so as not to direct his or her needs and longings to an actual parent or parental figure.

In this child's negative (or reversed) manifestation, he or she becomes the mama's boy or daddy's girl, who can't break the elementary bonds and thus is never satisfied. Or it becomes the melancholy dreamer. When this archetype is projected onto others, we feel neglected and unloved.

PAGE OF SWORDS AS HERO

This aspect of the child also characterizes the entire rank of knights who are moving from adolescence to adulthood. This child is aggressive and courageous, believing him- or herself invulnerable, while seeking conquests. He or she rights wrongs and rescues the weak.

In this child's negative (or reversed) manifestation, he or she becomes the inflated and abusive bully who takes dangerous risks. Or the child is the bullied coward who runs from confrontation. When this archetype is projected onto others, we feel lazy, invaded, run over, or we wait to be noticed and rescued.

PAGE OF PENTACLES AS PRECOCIOUS CHILD

The precocious or magical child is eager to learn, thoughtful, and demonstrates concentration and poise. He or she wants to know all about the world around it, and why things are the way they are.

In this child's negative (or reversed) manifestation, he or she becomes the know-it-all trickster and practical joker, or the slow and unresponsive dummy. When this archetype is projected onto others, we become bored and restless.

Reversed Court Cards

People rarely like receiving reversed court cards. The figures look uncomfortable and tradition says the people represented do not mean the querent well; a few go so far as to say they are evil people. However, most of us have never met a truly evil person, but rather people whose circumstances in or attitude toward life are in conflict with our own, creating disrupting or painful encounters. We all have our reversed days, times when we are angry or distraught, when everything we say comes out wrong, or when we are jealous or envious and even deliberately hurtful. This does not make us, or anyone else, bad or evil.

You do not ever have to use reversed cards, but using them does allow for a greater range of meanings and more precision. In the average ten-card reading, two of the cards (20 percent) will be from the court. It is not unusual to get anywhere from zero to four court cards. If you mix the deck thoroughly, top to bottom, then you can expect one or two reversed court cards with some regularity, while even three are not truly rare. Get used to them!

A reversed Queen of Swords, for example, may indicate hiding one's intellect and not letting others see your mental processes, thus suggesting an inner state or personality that no one else sees or knows. But all too often, reversed court cards seem "out of sorts." The Queen of Swords may not be thinking too clearly at the moment, or she has gone to the opposite extreme and is being excessively critical, or hyper-rational and lacking in good judgment. She may find that decisiveness eludes her. If this is your boss's temporary state, then try to get your job performance review re-scheduled. If it is your boss all the time, then you'll need a tough hide and the ability to make your own decisions; you might even find yourself fired and hired back a dozen times a day. If the reversed Queen of Swords represents a parental figure, you may have grown up with rules that didn't make much sense or that varied from day to day. You might have had to learn elsewhere how to set boundaries or find a different model for handling loss and pain without feeling victimized. If the card represents yourself, there may be a tendency to turn the hurt within and blame yourself for losses or, more rarely, to deny that something painful has even occurred.

If the position the queen occupies stands for "the gift" or "the best that can be achieved" or "advice," then we look to the benefits that can come from the Queen of Swords sheathing her sword. It suggests forgiving yourself and others for their mistakes. You should be gentle with critiques, giving others the benefit of the doubt and a second chance. You might offer to demonstrate what you mean (the open hand) rather than conveying everything in purely intellectual terms. It may be an opportunity to let people help you, to let down your guard, or to move beyond a stage of grieving—laying aside the widow's weeds. Focusing on the reversed symbols of the Waite-Smith card, the butterfly carved on the chair is uppermost, suggesting emerging from a cocoon of restriction into beautiful freedom. A reversed card in an advice position suggests that you *not* act as the upright figure would—at the same time it must still partake of its rank and suit.

Another way to think about reversed court cards is from the psychological perspective of what happens when someone's natural gifts and proclivities are not recognized, honored, or respected. Envision the Page of Cups as an imaginative, perhaps psychically open child. She has an imaginary friend and can see and hear things that others can't. If her parents and teachers tell her that she's lying or making things up, that nothing is there, and that she must never mention these experiences again, then what happens? She might repress her experiences. She could become overly introverted and turn away from external reality. Or she might accept herself as a liar and start acting this out. When her psychic experiences erupt they will probably do so in disturbing and inappropriate ways.

Imagine a co-worker who is a Knight of Pentacles reversed. It's almost impossible to get his cooperation with an innovative idea. He slows down every project and plays stupid practical jokes. What if all his life he wanted to be a farmer, but his family pressured him into computer technology? He just wants to be out in the sunshine, with his hands in the earth. We end up with a distorted, unfulfilled, unhappy Knight of Pentacles. Your problems with him could stem from his pent up frustration, and a lack of opportunity to express his true gifts.

Think of three or more well-known public personalities who are known for their "acting out": actors, sports figures, characters in books or film who would be called "bad boys or girls." Which reversed court cards would they be? Turn the card right-side up. What positive qualities might have been denigrated, repressed, or not allowed to develop, resulting in frustration and reactive behavior?

Think of one or two people in your life who've caused you grief at work, home, or among friends. Which reversed court cards are they? Turn the cards right-side up. What qualities should you look for in them that might bring out another side, a different response?

Reversed Court Card Reading

This spread uses only the court cards. Take a reversed court card from the exercise above, representing one of the people with whom you've experienced some difficulties. First, consider what this person's best qualities might be (the card upright). Then take the other court cards and shuffle them thoroughly, randomly turning some upside-down as you do so. Ask for advice indicating how you should act in relation to this person. Turn over the top card and put it to the left of the original, reversed card. If this new card is upright it indicates an overt, direct way that you can communicate with this person. If reversed, it suggests that you should not act towards this person as that card would do if upright. This card represents the primary way of acting.

Now, turn over the cards in the stack until you get to a reversed card (if your action card was upright) or an upright card (if your action card was reversed). The farther it is in the stack, the less strong its effectiveness. How does this second action card relate to the card of the other person? It represents a follow-up or supporting style to your first action.

Notice how the reversed significator relates to the other reversal. Turn both cards upright. What sort of relationship would they have? What keeps them from relating to each other productively?

REVERSED COURT CARD SPREAD

first upright	Significator	first reversed
card drawn	of a difficult	card drawn
SHOULD	person	**SHOULDN'T**
ACT LIKE	(a reversed	**ACT LIKE**
	card)	

EXAMPLE

Kathryn asked for a reading about the person to whom she was renting her basement apartment. She picked the King of Pentacles reversed from the RWS deck to represent Joseph, the renter. Although he was young, he was a professional chef, dark-haired, heavy-set, and uncommunicative. Upon moving in, he had sworn that he was very quiet and there would be few guests. In fact, he agreed to this in every discussion, and then completely ignored and flaunted their agreements—having people in and out in a steady stream all day and most of the night. When Kathryn turned the King of Pentacles upright she acknowledged that Joseph loved cooking and hospitality, and saw that he simply wanted to be a gracious host and lord of the manor to all his friends—only it was incredibly disrupting in her normally serene neighborhood. After shuffling, Kathryn turned up the King of Cups reversed. She felt it was saying that she should not act sympathetic and understanding toward him. To verify this, the next upright card she turned over was the upright Queen of Swords. This affirmed she should be absolutely firm about her boundaries and, if necessary, evict him, which the queen seemed quite prepared to do. When Kathryn examined the two kings next to each other, she could see that the King of Pentacles was not about to give an inch to the King of Cups—in fact, it looked like a passive-aggressive macho standoff. Interestingly, the next day, as Kathryn was preparing to give Joseph notice, he told her he would be moving out immediately, as if he had finally realized that he had reached her limit.

Reversed Card Keywords[2]

Keywords for reversed court cards, which can be used to modify upright interpretations, include:

Inner, vulnerable, reflective, magical, other-worldly, released, blocked, resisted, denied, rejected, unappreciated, immature, undeveloped, inappropriate, absent, insecure, inflated, arrogant, excessive, lacking, irresponsible, impotent or infertile, bullying, fatigued, frightened, stubborn, wounded, depressed, "acting out," misdirected, ineffectual, unfaithful, inconstant, foolish, broken through, or the upright qualities overturned.

Significators Revisited

The exercises in this chapter (and previous chapters) have provided opportunities to become more deeply acquainted with each of the court cards. Just like the process of getting to know new people, we've moved beyond first impressions to learn a lot more about what each court card is like: what they do, how they treat others, and what sort of personality they have. This is a good point to reexamine your choice of significator. A natural place to start is with the results of the personality quiz earlier in this chapter. Compare your results from taking the quiz for yourself with how you applied the categories to each of the court cards. Does one of the cards come especially close to "matching" your own personality? Which one? Is it the same card you chose as your significator in the introduction? You might also want to look at the roles and professions you assigned each card in chapter 3, and see if you find some matches there.

There is no single "correct" significator for yourself, or for anyone else. We all express each of the court card archetypes in different ways and at different times. The more you can see yourself in each of the court cards, the more easy it becomes to understand them and interpret their role in a reading. Remember that even if you don't use a formal significator in your spreads, the card you consider your main significator will have special import in readings.

ENDNOTES

1   Jana Riley's material on the court cards and the MBTI can be found in her book *Tarot Dictionary and Compendium*. Linda Gail Walters' material is available at http://members.cts.com/king/s/saoirse/TarotCourtCards.html.

2   See *The Complete Book of Tarot Reversals* by Mary K. Greer (St. Paul, MN: Llewellyn, 2002) for many more ways to read reversed cards.

CHAPTER FIVE

Court Card Relationships

People consult the Tarot for advice concerning personal relationships more than any other subject. The court cards can be especially illuminating in this context, because they reveal succinctly how people view themselves and others. Many of our subpersonalities are bound up with particular relationships. Friends, lovers, family members, and the people we work with all bring out different facets of our personality—and in so doing, reveal their own.

In relationships, there are both private and shared realities. The shared realities are the visible behaviors of the people involved: what they say, what they do. The private realities are internal to each person: desires and goals, feelings, and personal perceptions. We try to infer another's private reality from their visible behavior, and likewise, we may express what goes on inside us by our visible behaviors. Neither process is very reliable though. Even when we work hard to communicate clearly and honestly, we use personal filters that create twists in meaning.

The Tarot can help us recognize and compensate for some of these filters. Do you see your mother as the Queen of Swords, perhaps, and find her advice biting and cold? That perception, especially if you are not conscious of it, can keep you from understanding her motives and from appreciating how she sees you. When we see our own perceptions solidified in a Tarot image, they become easier to recognize, own, and deal with.

Friends and Family

List three or four people whom you know very well. Next to each person write the court card you most associate with that person.

Realize that each person has his or her own masks, roles, and subpersonalities just as you do. Now, consider which court card would each of these people have picked for themselves? How are your impressions of them different from how they would probably see themselves? If you get the opportunity, ask these people to pick a court card they feel most represents themselves. Find out why they picked that card. Compare with your choices for them.

Think of the person with whom you interact most in your life—a child, parent, friend, significant other, or someone at work or school. If you were to do daily readings involving this person he or she would appear on different days as different court cards. In fact, eventually you may be able to predict how that person is likely to relate to you on a given day, based on the court cards that appear in your readings.

Gail usually thought of her youthful husband Rick as the Knight of Wands, since he was a Sagittarius (fire sign) and always on the go. However, she found that when the King of Swords appeared in her daily readings, Rick would tend to be demanding and critical. When the Knight of Cups came up, Gail could expect sympathy and romance. When the Page of Swords presented itself (they had no children), it might refer to Rick in his wounded child moods. As she became more sensitive to this pattern, she began to see how much these were Rick's responses to her own issues and attitudes and that she could both anticipate his response and begin to modify her own attitudes that seemed to elicit these responses.

Rather than trying to guess which cards will mean what, take notes and observe in your actual readings what the cards signify. Only then see if you can then predict mood, style, attitude, actions, or focus of attention of your loved ones based on the different court cards that appear in situations in which they are involved.

The Influential Person Spread[1]

Using only the court cards, do a one-card reading on the question, "Who was the most important influence on my childhood development?" Decide whom this court card represents and how that person's personality is reflected in the card. Draw another card from the rest of the deck to represent the area of your life in which his or her influence has most affected you.

Projection

Jungian psychology provides a framework for integrating the court card as both yourself and as another person. This concept called "projection" refers to projecting (or thrusting) inner qualities of yourself onto other people around you, whether or not they have these qualities. They become shadowy mirror reflections of yourself. It works like this: you notice in other people some of the characteristics that you do not recognize in yourself—both positive and negative. As a result, you tend to let those people act out your own unconscious perceptions of yourself and your own inner situations, or you get angry with them when they don't.

Through the appearance of court cards in a spread, you can see what power and abilities you might be "giving away." What roles in your life do you expect other people to take on for you? These projections are especially strong across sexes—for example, when a man is discouraged from expressing his feminine side and finds a woman to act this out for him, and vice versa. Once you release others from these projections, you release them to be who they really are, and the same holds true for yourself.

Another form of projection is associated specifically with the shadow self—those negative inner qualities that we try to disown. The shadow is a person you would rather not be. Notice the actions that annoy you in other people. Have you ever acted likewise, or wanted to but left it to others? Whatever part of yourself you hide, will persist and take you unawares. Some of these projections are "bright shadows," that is, talents and abilities that you don't think you are worthy of. There are treasures locked away in each projection. Integrating both the positive and the negative consciously in yourself relieves you of tremendous burdens and releases strengths and abilities for your use.

Own your own projections!

If the querent is quick to identify a card as another person (particularly one the querent is struggling with), it is worth considering what the card may be saying about the querent's own personality. Although telling a querent "You're projecting!" probably is not the most diplomatic or helpful observation, it is important that readers be alert to the possibility and consider its impact on the interpretation. This is especially tricky when reading for oneself. One approach is to make a habit of always interpreting court cards as aspects of the person's own personality, even if it feels uncomfortable initially. You can always drop back to also seeing the card as someone else if that avenue of interpretation seems more productive.

Finally, it is often most helpful to be conscious of several layers of interpretation at once, rather than feeling the need to move to one and reject the others. There is always some element of projection in all our relationships, and the multilayered nature of the Tarot is one of its chief strengths as a divination tool. All Tarot cards, and court cards in particular, have a capacity to carry several complementary meanings at once. The more possibilities one can keep active in the imagination, the more likely it is that the meaning of the reading as a whole will crystallize around a helpful message.

Shadow Projection Exercise

STEP ONE

Separate out the sixteen court cards. Look through them and consciously pick a card faceup to represent a quality or characteristic you can't stand or don't like in others.

- Who most embodies this shadow quality? (This could be someone you know or a public figure.)

- How is this an aspect of yourself that destroys your relationships, kills your spirit, and keeps you from fulfilling your dreams? How does it tell you that you aren't okay?

Acknowledging this quality in yourself may be difficult, as you've probably spent a lifetime rejecting it. If you need help with this or with any of the questions below. Draw one card from the rest of the deck to help answer the question.

STEP TWO

Consciously pick a court card that shows how you want to appear to yourself and others instead of feeling unfulfilled, destructive, or not okay.

- How is this card a mask you wear to hide the shadow self? How is this mask an imposture?

STEP THREE

Return to the first card and answer the following questions:

- What lies have you been telling about who you are in order to hide this part of yourself?

- When you deny the shadow, you lessen what? Name an opposite and worthy attribute. (For example, if you deny prejudice, then acceptance may be an opposite.)

- What does this card want or intend? If in doubt, ask a figure on the card what it wants.

- How are you expending energy to keep the shadow elements below the surface?

- How can you unmask or reveal this part of yourself? How can you accept this deepest, darkest aspect of yourself?

- What gifts does your shadow hold for you?

- What would need to happen for it to be okay to be your shadow self?

STEP FOUR

Look through the entire deck faceup and consciously pick a card (not a court card) that expresses this. Then turn the deck over, shuffle, fan the cards, and pick one more card at random to express the same thing. What do these two cards—one consciously picked and one selected at random—recommend that you do?

- Whom does the other person become—the one on whom you projected these qualities—if you take back your projection?

Guides, Teachers, and Mentors

Each of the court card personalities (especially when seen as archetypes, as described in chapter 4) can manifest in our lives as people who teach us about an unacknowledged or unexplored aspect of ourselves. They become role models for how to think and act or, in negative manifestations, how not to think and act. Whenever you get a court card in a spread position but feel inadequate to express it, ask yourself what it has to teach you. Is there someone in your life whose skills, personality, or style would be a model for either correct action or action to avoid? What does this figure recommend that you do?

Contacting an Inner Teacher Court Card

To find your inner teacher, look for the court card corresponding to the sign in which your moon is found, or you can be even more specific and use the decanate association as given in chapter 6 (page 123). If you don't have this information, or if you would prefer, you can choose a card that you feel best represents your inner teacher, or allow a court card to come to you spontaneously in the meditation exercise that follows.

Lay out all sixteen court cards and pick the figure you feel most drawn to as a teacher—a personality you could rely on for inner direction regarding your highest potential in any given area. Take a moment to sit quietly with this personality; ask your higher self if there are any objections to this teacher. If you do not feel a strong "no" or any sense of discomfort, then go ahead with the exercise. In their book *Spirit Guides: Access to Inner Worlds*, Mike Samuels and Hal Bennett have some good advice for checking the information you receive during a visioning, more specifically, they explain how to see if the advice is from a "spiritual" source, or if it is what they call "ego static." It may be summed up this way:

1. Are your muscles relaxed and do you feel at ease? (Spiritual)

2. Is the information nonjudgmental? (Spiritual)

3. Is it harmful toward none? (Spiritual)

4. Is it based on love? (Spiritual)

5. Does it please or gratify you? (If so, it it may be your ego speaking.)

6. Does it bring out your inner doubts and fears? (It may be a negative shadow speaking.)

Have your Tarot journal at hand. Place the court card representing your inner teacher in front of you. Look at it carefully then close your eyes and see it in your mind's eye. Open your eyes and check the details, then close your eyes again until you can reproduce it as precisely as possible in your mind's eye. Relax all your muscles and begin deep, even breathing, concentrating on allowing your stomach to expand with each inhalation and contract with each exhalation.

See yourself as a tree sending roots into the earth, deeper and deeper until they enter a cave in the center of the earth. Then, imagine you are descending down into the cave through the taproot, as if it were an elevator. Look around at the walls, floor, colors, and furnishings of the cave. Become aware of temperature, smells, textures. Don't worry if your impressions are vague and you don't actually "see" anything. You may also make up an imaginary environment.

Your inner teacher approaches and kisses you on your forehead to open your inner sight and to bless and protect you; then he or she touches your heart to make you receptive only to thoughts coming from love. Observe your inner teacher; watch how the environment around this teacher changes and intensifies in color, shape, sound, and texture. Don't worry if you have difficulty "seeing." Use all your senses on the inner plane—feel for any subtle change, notice reactions in your own body. Often certain symbols, images, and impressions will appear around the figure or will flash through your consciousness. Note them.

Now ask your teacher any questions you want answered, for example:

- What do you have to teach me?
- How can I best use the Tarot?
- What do I need to do at this time to develop my Tarot skills?
- Which court card represents an aspect of myself that I most need to bring to consciousness?
- What is the meaning of [*insert a particular card or symbol*]?

You can also ask to be guided to other helpers for assistance in healing, relationships, work, creativity, past or future lives, or political and global understanding.

When you've finished, thank your inner teacher. Take a moment to simply be in gratitude and accept any last awarenesses that come to you. Rise back up along your taproot, bringing your consciousness into your physical body. When you are ready, open your eyes on an exhalation while saying your name aloud to yourself.

Upon your return, write down all impressions. Describe the appearance of your inner teacher, the cave, your questions, the responses, and any images or scenes that flashed through your mind—no matter how irrelevant they seem.

Court Card Dialogs

Finding several court cards in a reading suggests there are a number of people with different needs or agendas involved in the situation, or that different aspects of the self want different things. Sometimes both are happening simultaneously. You may be involved with people who encourage, support, or model the different sides of yourself.

Dialogs allow each figure to state his or her own ideas and opinions, to tell what they want and why, and to give advice. A court card figure can speak to the querent or to another card. It can reveal rights and wrongs in any given situation. Several personalities can brainstorm much more effectively than just one because you will get multiple perspectives and styles.

The conversations and exchanges of ideas arising from dialogs can be excellent preparation for encounters with the real people they represent. Because the words in a dialog come from you, you are likely to be more open to, and understanding of, the other person's point of view. They also allow you to vent frustrations, say or hear things that inhibitions or social convention might not allow, and reveal truths you would not otherwise have acknowledged.

Each court card in a reading has the potential of being an inner teacher. Asking them what they would do about any other card in a reading or any aspect of your situation can open up new possibilities or insights. If you like what one of them recommends, ask it to be your guide as you handle the situation, and bring that subpersonality to the forefront when required.

There is no reason why a Tarot reader can't ask the querent in the middle of a reading, "What would the Knight of Wands, in a near-future position, recommend that you do about the Five of Swords in the environment position?" In this case, one person has all the swords and two people are walking away. The Knight of Wands doesn't seem like the type that would run away and yet he seems to have more compassion than the person with all the swords. His horse and armor give him an advantage and his cheerful nature might alleviate some of the gloom—but it all depends on what the person getting the reading sees at the moment.

Dialogs can be between a person and a card or among several cards. Whether writing them down or speaking them, it is helpful to follow a few guidelines:

- Write dialogs as if they were movie screenplays, with lines identified by speaker. If you are writing really fast, then use dashes or an initial to show a change of speaker.

- Write, type, or speak continuously. Try not to think about it, but come out with the first thing that comes to mind. If you are writing, try to keep the pen moving and don't worry about handwriting, spelling, or grammar.

- To break the ice, start out with the silliest thing you can imagine. The conversation will naturally deepen as it goes along.

- Notice pictorial images that flash in your head (usually memory snapshots) and try to integrate them.

- Literalize objects and the environments of the cards. Ask what the figure is doing with objects that appear on the cards.

- Try to create a real interchange. All the figures, human or otherwise, can both ask and answer questions. Let them challenge and argue with you and/or each other.

- Imagine a character from one card entering the environment of another card. What happens?

Dialog Exercises

- Get your Tarot journal or some paper and a pen. Shuffle your deck and turn over cards from the top, placing the first minor arcana number card and the first two court cards in front of you. Imagine that the court cards are involved together in the situation depicted by the number card. Write down the scene as if it were a play script.

- Use any reading you've done that contains at least one court card. Discuss with that court card figure about what it thinks of the situation and how you should handle it. If there is more than one court card, get the opinion of each of the figures separately. Have them debate their opinions. Is one of them more convincing to you than the other? Whose advice would you prefer to follow?

- Use a reading in which three or more court cards appear. Think of them as an inner committee. Give each of these inner parts of yourself a descriptive name (i.e., the critic, couch potato, inner dad, your baby name, etc.). Call a committee meeting, and find out what each part wants and needs. Can you find a way for each part to get something it wants—sometimes it just wants to be heard—so that in exchange it will agree to work with the overall plan?

- You might want to keep the idea of dialogs in mind as you read through the section on elemental dignities in chapter 6. There are lots of suggestions about how figures from different suits and elements might support, challenge or interfere with each other, and what their attitudes might be toward each other.

Relationship Spread

This spread helps clarify relationship issues between two people. It is ideal to have both people present to interpret the spread. The relationship can be of any type. Shuffle the deck and place the seven cards facedown, as illustrated on the facing page:

RELATIONSHIP SPREAD

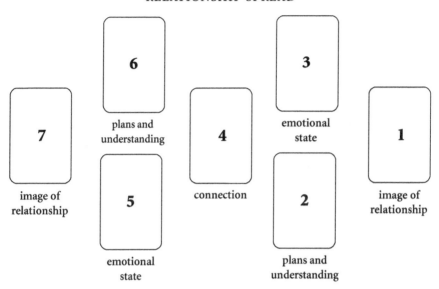

- Cards 1, 2, and 3 refer to person A; cards 5, 6, and 7 refer to person B. Card 4 refers to the relationship itself, the point of connection between the two people. Turn the cards faceup in order, except for card 4, which should remain facedown until last.

- Card 1 is person A's image of the relationship. What appears here is often a self-image or an extreme interpretation of the relationship (either overidealized or a paranoid, worst-case scenario). If the relationship were a play with person A as director, this is the scene or character that would be center stage, under the spotlight.

- Card 2 is person A's conscious plans and verbalized understanding of the relationship. When person A tries to be analytical and approach the relationship objectively, this is what comes out. Note the differences between this card and card 1, which reflects the subconscious or "automatic" perceptions, rather than the mental constructions of card 2.

- Card 3 is person A's emotional state in the relationship. The contrast between cards 3 and 2 is the contrast between heart and mind. Both draw on the perception shown in card 1, but process the image in different ways.

- Card 5 is person B's emotional state in the relationship. Comparing this card with card 3 gives insight into the emotional dynamic between the two people.

- Card 6 is person B's conscious plans and verbal understanding of the relationship. When the two people talk and negotiate together, it is cards 2 and 6 interacting.

- Card 7 is person B's image of the relationship. Note how it feeds into the thoughts and feelings (cards 6 and 5) and also how it compares with A's image of things (card 1). Are the two images of the relationship compatible, or are they directing plays with two different scripts?

- Card 4 is the connection between the two people, a lesson for their higher selves to work with to make the relationship successful. This card may show the overarching theme of the relationship, it may represent a challenge to be engaged, or a word of advice. Often, progress can be made if each person moves out of their private image of the relationship (cards 1 and 7) to engage the common issue represented in this card. To connect emotionally (imagine a line from card 3 to card 5) as well as verbally (imagine a line from card 2 to card 6), the two people must pass through this intersection point.

The three cards for each person give some insight into their inner worlds at the moment, in the context of the relationship. At the conclusion of the reading, each person (with the help of the reader) should identify a court card that might have the same subconscious, emotional, and mental qualities that were described in the spread. Sometimes, an appropriate court card already appears in the spread itself. More often, you will need to look through the deck and find one. Place the court cards for each person on either side of card 4 and set the other cards of the spread aside. How does each of the two court cards relate to card 4? (Note which direction they are facing, and their level of interest.) How can the two court cards use card 4 as a common ground?

The Ethics of Relationship Readings

Certain ethical issues arise when a reading involves someone who is not present. Many readers refuse to do a reading about someone without his or her permission. One reason for this involves privacy concerns. The cards might reveal certain aspects of the person's life he or she would rather not have known.

More subtle issues also arise when the querent asks for insight into another person's life—a spouse or lover, perhaps, or a child. The querent is likely to project their own hopes and fears about the person onto the cards. Problem cards may assume tragic proportions or be rejected as inaccurate. The querent may have unfair or unhelpful perceptions of the absent party, which the reader inadvertently encourages and reinforces by taking them at face value during the reading. In addition to privacy concerns, there is now also the risk of being drawn into a gossipy conversation about a third party. This can be especially awkward if the reader knows the absent party.

Without the other person's permission, there are also spiritual and karmic concerns about interfering in that other person's life uninvited.

One way to mitigate some of these ethical concerns is always keep the querent as the primary subject of the reading. Instead of doing a reading about the querent's spouse, do a reading about the querent's marriage, focusing on the relationship rather than the other party. Or you can focus on what the querent wants and needs in a relationship. Although a reading focused on the querent's relationship or personal needs can still offer insight into what the other party is bringing into the picture, that information now appears in the context of the querent's own perceptions, choices, and feelings.

It is also helpful to remember (and articulate, if necessary) that Tarot is a personal medium—it is strongly influenced by the reader, querent, and other people who may be present and participating in the reading. So insights that arise regarding an absent party "belong" to the querent and reader. Different facets of the situation would appear if the absent party were having his or her own reading on the same subject. A relationship reading describes how other persons bear on the querent's situation, not how they are outside that context.

And, of course, the usual caveats about staying within one's area of expertise apply in relationship readings. Tarot readers should not give medical or legal advice (unless they also have training and qualifications in these areas). Relationship counseling, obviously, is a more ambiguous matter because the querent expects to extract some helpful advice from a Tarot consultation. Still, it is important to recognize when a querent's needs would be better served by a family counseling specialist, for example.

Finding the Couples in the Tarot Court[2]

The members of one suit are not necessarily attracted to the other members of their suit. Many of them appear more attracted to other court cards. Who is having an affair with whom? Your task is to find the couples. Line up all the court cards and move them around until you find pairs that seem to be drawn to each other. Once you have them paired up, tell their stories. Relationship nuances may arise based on the directions in which the figures face. How does moving them back-to-front (moving the figure to the left or the right) change their dynamics?

For instance, in the Marseilles deck, the King of Coins and Queen of Swords have a mature, considered relationship. The Queen of Wands is dallying with the Knight of Wands (who is bisexual and having an affair with the Page of Swords). The King of Wands is seeing the young and frivolous maiden, Page of Chalices (who is at the start of her career as a grand courtesan). The King of Swords and Queen of Chalices really have the hots for each other. Meanwhile the Knight of Chalices longs after his queen, but his love goes unrequited. The Page of Wands and Knight of Coins have a platonic (men-at-arms) relationship, but the knight's younger brother, the Page of Coins, is still jealous. The King of Chalices and Queen of Coins have a marriage of convenience. She indulges his moods and drinking, and he respects her business acumen, which allows him to be so self-indulgent. The Knight of Swords is jealous of everyone else's happiness. (See cards on facing page.)

Couples from the Ancient Tarots of Marseilles

The People-Card Reading

This is a simple two-card reading, yet it is helpful in understanding the changing dynamics of an ongoing relationship, or to gain a quick insight into why certain people come briefly into your life. You can also discover things about yourself that you were never consciously aware of before. Use it for all kinds of relationships: family, friends, co-workers, teachers, lovers, and between different parts of yourself. It can be expanded for more information, as I'll describe later.

Using only the sixteen court cards, you will choose one card to tell you what qualities you are currently learning from a particular person at this time. Then you will choose a second card to tell you what qualities they are learning from you. The resulting cards show how these people currently appear to you and how you appear to them. If there is a disparity between the qualities the cards describe and your perception of yourself, ask yourself why you are unaware of these qualities.

Although you can do this reading by yourself, you will gain more insight as to how it works if you first try it with a friend. Each of you randomly picks a court card representing what you are learning from the other. Then tell your partner what you are learning from him or her, based on the card you drew. You may be very surprised by what they see in you. They might perceive qualities you've never seen in yourself. Once you have experienced this with a friend, you will be better prepared to understand what the cards portend when you do it alone.

Shuffle all sixteen court cards, then spread them in a fan, facedown.

1. With your left hand, pick a card to represent the qualities you are learning from the other person. Place this card to the left.

2. With your right hand, pick a card to represent the qualities they are learning from you. Place this card to the right of the first card.

For each person, draw three more cards to discover the kind of situations from which each of you experience your learning opportunity. They show the developmental stages of your interaction and learning:

1. How it was

2. The current situation

3. Its future potential

Blend the meanings of the cards until they seem to describe a recognizable situation or interplay in your relationship.

Group Dynamics

Most of our relationships aren't singular, but are based on a constantly shifting dynamic among all the people in a group.

Group Relationship Spread[3]

Take out the sixteen court cards. Select a significator for yourself. List all the people (up to fifteen) in a particular group whose relationship interests you. These could be members of your family, co-workers, friends, project members, or significant others of any kind. Number and set up positions corresponding to the numbers in a circular layout around your significator.

Shuffle the rest of the court cards (leaving out your significator)and deal them randomly into these positions. Examine them to see their different roles and attitudes. Is your father a dependent page? Is a child a tyrant king? Who's looking at whom and who's looking away? Who's in the same suits and who's in conflicting suits?

If you want to expand on this reading, take the remainder of the deck, shuffle, cut, and deal one card adjacent to each of the court cards. This card shows the relationship issues or communications you may have with the person, or it can give advice on how to interact with them. Draw one additional card at random and place it next to your significator to show how you are feeling or reacting in general.

Multiple Court Cards

The number of court cards of the same rank that appear in a reading can be significant, often suggesting a particular relationship among people—usually peers of some kind or, as always, aspects of the self. Preset meanings can be stilted and don't always apply, so consider what other possibilities can give additional richness to your interpretations.

Kings

Multiple kings: Public recognition, publicity, being honored, a business meeting, stultification, conflicting "shoulds" and "oughts."

Two kings: A partnership, profitable contract or deal, conflicting opinions.

Three kings: Unexpected meetings, great success, much authority, treaties.

Four kings: Tremendous power, struggles for control, complications through blinding conceit or hubris, great limitations, absolute boundaries.

No kings: Lack of decisiveness, power, and outer authority; now may not be the time to act.

Queens

Multiple queens: Gossip, coffee klatch, women's group, envy, possessiveness.

Two queens: Friend, acquaintance, rival, conflicting needs.

Three queens: Powerful and influential friends, sympathy, enmity, cattiness.

Four queens: Authority and influence, great culture and refinement, complications through excessive introversion, too many caretakers.

No queens: Lack of introspection, nurturing, sensitivity, or understanding.

Knights

Multiple knights: Lots of movement, high energy and dynamism, sports, military, training.

Two knights: A legal or court case, protection, rivalry, conflicting missions.

Three knights: Rank and honor, dominance struggles, development in different directions, compatriots.

Four knights: Meetings with the great, complications, situation out of control, high testosterone, war.

No knights: Extremely slow development of situation, not much movement or action.

Pages

Multiple pages: Children, new ideas and plans, conflicting needs, play, learning.

Two pages: Friendship, sharing, exchange, competition, conflicting interests or focuses.

Three pages: Society of the young, allies.

Four pages: Elementary school, elementary stages, struggle getting off the ground, excessive slowness, extreme naïveté.

No pages: Absence of friends or children; lack of humility, freshness, or playfulness.

Combinations

King and knight: Delegation of responsibility, mentoring, direction, palace revolt, challenge, attraction.

King or queen and page: Teaching, parent/child interaction, relationship with a great age or role difference.

King and queen: Attraction, a couple, possibly well-established or long-term relationship, parents.

Queen and knight: Affair, romance, courtly love tradition, proving worthiness, being set on a quest.

One queen and several knights or kings or vice versa: A choice among lovers, competition for favors, rivalry, jealousy, multiple ways of acting or attitudes toward someone.

Several knights and pages: School, college, fraternity, academy, gang, athletics.

Dream Selves

Select a dream that you would like to explore. List each person who appeared in the dream. Include animals that seem like they could be people. Consciously choose a court card to correspond with each of these dream people, including the "you" in your dream. While dreams may depict actual human relationships, each dream character is also an aspect of yourself. Use the court card to determine what part of yourself each dream figure represents. (Check your list of roles, masks, and sub-personalities from chapter 4.)

Draw additional cards at random from the remainder of the deck to get more information about what this figure is doing in your dream. You can also draw cards to elucidate other dream symbols and events.

ENDNOTES

1   Spread used with permission. Teresa Michelsen is author of *Creating Your Own Tarot Spreads* in the Llewellyn Special Topics in Tarot series.

2   Leave it to the French to realize that not everyone is paired with members of their own suit. This exercise originated in with Marie LeConte of Paris, France, who taught it to Rachel Pollack.

3   Spread used with permission. This basic format of this spread comes from Tarot reader and teacher Fern Mercier of Auckland, New Zealand.

CHAPTER SIX

The Court and the Cosmos

So far, we have focused on the court cards as people or as qualities that people show. Yet they can also be seen in more metaphysical terms. (Metaphysics is the branch of philosophy that asks questions about the true nature of things.) Many spiritual traditions have maintained that the same underlying principles appear in human affairs (the microcosm) as in the cosmos as a whole (the macrocosm), and that to affect one is to affect the other. This point of view is expressed succinctly in the Hermetic saying "As above, so below."

Modern science has sought the underlying principles of the cosmos reductively, analyzing complicated systems into their component parts and identifying laws that govern how the parts behave. From this perspective, the connection between the person and the cosmos is that both are composed of the same fundamental building blocks (the subatomic particles), which interact through the same fundamental forces.

Many spiritual traditions, however, have sought the underlying principles of the cosmos by thinking analogically, rather than reductively. From this perspective, the connection between the person and the cosmos is one of symbolic parallels. We may see reflections of ourselves and our qualities in the forces of nature, in the motions of the planets, or in the plants and animals around us. Different metaphysical systems have been developed because different cultures see these parallels in different ways. These systems also incorporate the culture's religious and mystical traditions.

We have already emphasized one of the oldest metaphysical systems in the European tradition: the four elements of fire, water, air, and earth. These are not just different substances, as we are likely to regard them today. To the ancients, they represented the primal qualities that all things partake of. They apply to human personalities as readily as to phenomena in the outer world. The concept of the four elements thoroughly permeates metaphysical thinking in the Western world, playing key roles in astrology, Qabalah, and magic.

Ancient peoples saw metaphysical meaning everywhere, in the natural world, in the human personality, and even in the structures of society. Many Indo-European cultures, from places as far-flung as Ireland and India, had cosmologies anchored in the four elements. The world was believed to be made of up sky, water, and land, with fire as a sacred element that was central to the well-being of the people and a special prerogative of kings. These cultures also frequently recognized three castes or classes of people, each with its own function: the priests, the warriors, and the farmers. The king was again a central figure, with obligations to the other three. Interestingly, warriors were usually associated with the waters, although modern Tarot users would be more inclined to place them with swords and air (sky).

Neoplatonism

In western European culture, one of the most influential metaphysical systems, Neoplatonism, developed out of the teachings of Plato and Neoplatonic scholars, who elaborated on Plato's ideas through the course of many centuries. Although the roots of Neoplatonism are pre-Christian, the philosophy was adapted to fit a Christian worldview, and Neoplatonic ideas were incorporated in Christian theology.

For Plato, mind is a more fundamental reality than matter. A single, divine mind lies behind all of creation, pure, simple, and perfect. The gap between the changeless, eternal simplicity of the divine mind and the complex, strikingly imperfect realities of earthly existence was so great that intermediate stages were needed to connect the one with the other. Plato's realm of ideal forms was one such intermediary level. The forms were mental abstractions, like the idea of a perfect equilateral triangle, or like the idea of a perfect human being. We connect with the world of forms, not through our senses, which reveal only the many imperfect approximations found in the material world, but through contemplation and abstract thought.

Neoplatonic philosophers posited many different levels of reality, through which divine thought became increasingly complex and concrete, ultimately manifesting as material, earthly bodies at the lowest and final level. Neoplatonism offered a theoretical basis for the study of astrology. The stars and planets, pure heavenly lights, moving in their changeless, predictable cycles, were high up on the progression from matter to mind, and so watching their motions was something akin to peering into the mind of God.

It is quite possible that the major arcana of the Tarot were designed with a Neoplatonic conception of the cosmos in mind, since this model was pivotal to early Renaissance thinking in northern Italy. At the least, there seems to be a progression from the all-too-mundane Fool to the religious symbolism of the World card (which is actually referred to as "God the Father" in a fifteenth-century manuscript). A similar progression is apparent in the ordinary human figures (such as the Pope and Emperor) near the beginning, and loftier celestial subjects (such as the Star, the Moon, and the Sun) near the end. Scholars have yet to find an explicit match between the Tarot and any particular metaphysical system, however, so such possibilities, although suggestive, remain in the realm of speculation.

The Neopagan Cosmology

Since the late 1960s there has been an ongoing modern renaissance of Tarot studies and new decks that seems to be still gaining in momentum. Accompanying this has been the growth of what may be called a neopagan movement or more specifically, a blend of modern pagan witchcraft and a more political, Earth-based eco-feminism, with practices based on magic, divination, and ritual. Neopaganism has become a syncretic spiritual movement, some say the first truly new religion to emerge in modern times, with a myriad of forms and relatively few basic tenets beyond a belief in the sacredness of the natural world; divinity (often polytheistic) that is male and female and can be found within the individual; and the Wiccan Rede that states, "as ye harm none, do as ye will."[1] Many decks have been and are being designed with this consciousness in mind. These are the decks that look to plants, animals, and sacred places as alternatives to traditional court cards. Suits may be named for natural phenomena, like flame, wave, wind, and earth.[2] Styles and interests range from a resurrection of pre-Christian traditions to an evolutionary bent toward new forms, technologies, and space travel.

The Neopagan emphasis on the goddess often makes for fundamentally different cosmological assumptions. The goddess is viewed as an immanent deity bound to the cycles of earthly life. Hence symbols such as the changing seasons or the phases of the moon, cycles in which all phases are equally valued, replace the "ladder to heaven" hierarchies of the more patriarchal cosmologies. This is often accompanied by a rejection of hierarchies in social arrangements as well; instead, the dominant metaphor becomes the circle of an intimate community.

One of the founding organizations of this modern movement, Gardnerian Witchcraft, although it used the Golden Dawn as a major source, has as its central ritual the sacred marriage of the god and goddess, in which the chalice and the blade are the primary symbols. Thus, the merging of water and fire appear as the sword within the cup, and some pagan decks, such as the *Nigel Jackson Tarot*, have swords as fire, cups as water, wands as air, and pentacles as earth. There is no "pagan consensus" on these correspondences, though, and many pagan decks equate swords with air and wands with fire.

Tarot Correspondences

Qabalah and astrology are the two metaphysical systems, besides the elements, that have been applied most intensively to the Tarot. There is no single "right way" to make such connections, therefore many different systems of correspondences have been proposed. In this book, we give special attention to that used by the Hermetic Order of the Golden Dawn, because it has been the most influential in the English-speaking Tarot world for about a century. The Golden Dawn was founded in London in 1888 as an organization of men and women who practiced ceremonial magic for the purpose of purifying one's individual nature so as to bring it into communication with one's "Holy Guardian Angel" (or higher self).

Other systems and metaphysical perspectives are also used, and new ones are still being invented. A system is usually best used with a deck designed with that system in mind, and it may not translate well to other decks. In continental European tradition, the correspondences of the French Tarot writers, such as Eliphas Lévi, are more widely followed than those of the Golden Dawn, but rarely do the alternatives give much attention to the minor arcana number and court cards. More recently, John Opsopaus, for example, has done an impressive job of applying Pythagorean numerology, Greek philosophy, and alchemical principles to the Tarot majors and minors.[3]

The Golden Dawn established correspondences between the Tarot and as many different magical models as possible—this is the strength of the Golden Dawn system. Thus the Tarot became a method of easily relating all spheres of experience at several different levels of reality. To use these ideas most effectively, you should work with a Golden Dawn- or Thoth-based Tarot deck. The core systems they associated with the Tarot were:

- Western magical Qabalah and Tree of Life

    —the Tetragrammaton (four-letter name of God)

    —the four worlds

    —the ten sephiroth

    —the twenty-two paths (not applicable to the court cards)

- Astrology

    —planets

    —signs of the zodiac

    —decans (ten degree segments of the zodiac)

- Celestial navigation

    —stars

    —quadrants of the heavens

- Numerology

- Elemental theory

    —Western, Greek-based elements

    —Eastern, tattwas (includes geometric forms and colors)

- Angelic/Enochian (based on the angelic language of John Dee)[4]
- I Ching hexagrams and geomancy (added later by Aleister Crowley)

Although these metaphysical systems are all different, what they have in common is a view of the cosmos that organizes our experiences, both physical and spiritual, into universal categories. These categories are reflected not only in the external world, but within our consciousness as well. The Tarot, too, can be seen as a metaphysical system, a map of the underlying structure of things. When we see the Tarot in this light, the court cards take on a more expansive role. Besides representing people or personality traits, they are also windows on the underlying nature of our life and our world as we experience them.

For the Tarot reader, this understanding can give more possibilities, and more depth, to the court cards and their meanings. For example, in the Golden Dawn system where the princesses are associated with the Qabalistic sephirah of Malkuth, the appearance of a princess in a reading may suggest that something long imaged and planned may become manifest and take physical form. The card may still carry a meaning connected with the querent's personality style or relationships, but it now also taps into larger issue of what the cosmos is bringing forth, and how the querent is active in that creative process.

We will only look at those categories which can be easily understood and most helpful to Tarot card readings.

The Qabalah

Qabalah (also Cabala, Kabbalah) are Hebrew mystical teachings that first began as an oral tradition, the word "qabalah" itself meaning "mouth to ear." By the thirteenth century, core Qabalistic teachings appeared in books including the *Sepher Zohar* ("Book of Splendor") and *Sepher Yetzirah* ("Book of Creation"). Qabalah study was likened to entering a splendid but dangerous garden, and was not advised before one's fortieth year. Christians who studied it believed it demonstrated the coming of Christ and therefore could be a tool for converting Jews (which legitimized its adoption by Christians). Soon

Christian writings became the basis for a Western magical Qabalah that focused on the process of creation as described in the diagram or model known as the Tree of Life.

Like Neoplatonism, Qabalah embodies an *emanationist* philosophy, meaning material creation emerging from divine consciousness through a series of intermediary stages. In Qabalah, there are ten of these stages, called *sephiroth* or spheres. Each sephirah (the singular of sephiroth) has its own unique qualities, and we see these qualities reflected in ourselves and throughout the cosmos. The relationships between the ten sephiroth are illustrated in the Tree of Life diagram (see page 115). With its ten sephiroth and twenty-two connecting paths, it is considered a blueprint for understanding all things. Sometimes called the "ladder of lights," the tree depicts the emanation of God's qualities into the material world and humanity's path back to God.

- Kether is the first and highest of the sephiroth, closest to God. It is pure being, eternal and undifferentiated. Astrologically, it corresponds with "First Swirlings" or the Big Bang.

- Chokmah is the second sephirah. It represents primal energy, the force of creation and change that initiates creation. It corresponds with the whole zodiac.

- Binah is the third sephirah. It gives shape to things by channeling the energy of creation into specific patterns. (One might think of Binah as responsible for creating the ideal forms in Plato's system.) It corresponds with Saturn.

- Chesed, the fourth, benevolently multiplies possibilities and is responsible for growth. We have reached a less abstract level, because now new things are coming into being and changing with time. It corresponds with Jupiter.

- Geburah, the fifth, is restrictive, eliminating some possibilities, causing them to die or wither. It corresponds with Mars.

- Tiphareth, the sixth, represents balanced consciousness, the individual's higher self, halfway between the divine consciousness of Kether and the purely world-focused approaches of the lower sephiroth. It corresponds with the sun.

- Netzach, the seventh, is the energy of feelings and emotions, world-focused passions, and the force of attraction. It corresponds with Venus.

- Hod, the eighth, is mental, verbal energy, associated with communication, structure, and reasoning. It corresponds with Mercury.

- Yesod, the ninth, is imagination, through which we form and prepare to manifest our pictures of the world. It corresponds with the moon.

- Malkuth, the tenth and final sephirah, is the material world itself, where ideas come into full physical existence. It corresponds with Earth.

The conceptions of the ten sephiroth have changed through the centuries, of course, and they are viewed differently by different interpreters. These brief descriptions summarize the Qabalistic ideas that have informed the design of Tarot decks such as the Waite-Smith, Thoth, Golden Dawn and other similar but more recent decks.

Soul Nexus Spread

This spread draws on the Tree of Life to focus on the place where microcosm and macrocosm meet, Tiphareth and the surrounding four sephiroth.

- Shuffle the entire deck and lay out the cards in the order indicated, facedown. Reveal them in reverse order, beginning with position 5 and working upward. You can also use your significator as the card in position 3.

- Position 1 is Chesed. It indicates the positive, creative cosmic forces that are at work in the querent's life. These are gifts, blessings, and new beginnings. These are not things the querent is necessarily trying to arrange, but instead come "out of the blue." The reader should focus on the more positive meanings of the card that appears here.

- Position 2 is Geburah. It indicates the negative, restrictive cosmic forces that are at work in the querent's life. These are challenges, losses, and difficult transitions. Again, these are not generally planned events—the querent's role is in responding to them. The reader should emphasize the problematic meanings of the card that appears here.

- Position 3 is Tiphareth. This shows what the querent needs to focus on to maintain perspective and stay centered.

- Position 4 is Netzach. This represents the querent's emotional state and reactions. There is often a close connection between Netzach and Geburah, with Netzach showing a reaction to Geburah. Tiphareth may need to "intercede" between the two to help replace automatic responses with more thoughtful ones.

- Position 5 is Hod. This represents the structures the querent is trying to impose on the situation. This can be a response to the gifts from Chesed, as one tries to process what has been given and focus it into a plan. Again, Tiphareth may offer useful insights on how to accomplish this, and avoid having our mental machinations become too restrictive and narrow.

SOUL NEXUS SPREAD

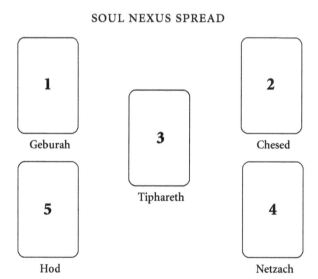

Geburah

Chesed

Tiphareth

Hod

Netzach

To use this spread in a more metaphysical style, examine the flow of energy from Chesed down to Hod, passing through each sephirah in order. How is the energy being altered, shaped, and made more specific and personal as it descends? Tiphareth is a place of objectivity. Is it possible to stand there, in the center, unmoved, and survey the surrounding situations, nonjudgmentally, nondefensively, accepting both good and bad with a neutral, calm awareness?

The Golden Dawn Qabalistic Correspondences

The Tree of Life is a diagram (facing page) of the stages of creation, but it is also a diagram of the human personality. The paths connecting the different sephiroth (twenty-two in all, one for each letter of the Hebrew alphabet) represent ways for us to move from one level of consciousness to another. Traditionally, each path is associated with a card of the major arcana. This fits nicely with the idea that the major arcana represent major life lessons that help us to grow and learn.

The Golden Dawn associated the number cards with the sephiroth themselves, assigning the four aces to Kether, the four twos to Chokmah, and so on. These assignments strongly influenced the card meanings and symbolism of many modern decks. The fives of each suit, for example, appear negative or tragic in many decks, because the sephirah Geburah corresponds with Mars and thus presides over death, loss, and the "pruning" of life's possibilities.

The Golden Dawn also assigned the court cards to four of the sephiroth. The Shekhinah, or female presence of the living God, is lodged in the sphere of Sovereignty (Malkuth, the tenth sephirah), which is also the material world. This is a fitting place for the princess. Seen Qabalistically, the Shekhinah is also the wise Mother, the third sephirah, Understanding (Binah), on the tree. So Malkuth is in affinity with the princess and Binah with the queen. Both feminine court cards correspond to the Hebrew letter *He* in the Tetragrammaton, since they are the same being in two different manifestations. The king (Thoth knight) lodges in Chokmah, primal energy, and the force of creation and the balance pole for Binah, while the prince (traditional knight) is found in the center sephirah, Tiphareth, the position of the astrological sun and the sacrificed son.[5] (Recall from chapter 2 that the Golden Dawn regarded the fiery, active knights of traditional decks as the "true" kings, and reduced the sedentary kings to the rank of prince.)

THE QABALISTIC TREE OF LIFE

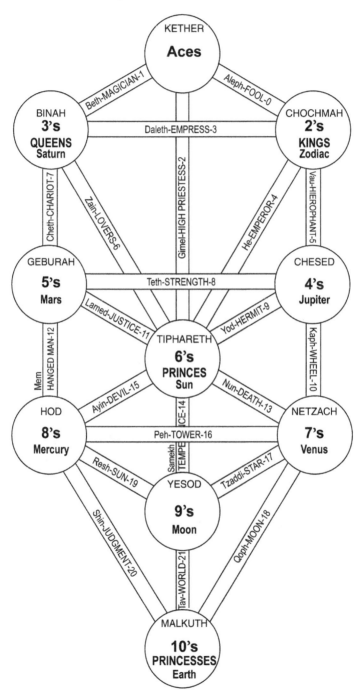

Since court cards share places on the Tree of Life with the number cards, each court card is connected with a number card of the same suit. The Queen of Swords, for instance, corresponds with the airy part of the third sephirah, Binah, and thus the Three of Swords. The Princess of Pentacles would correspond with the Ten of Pentacles. These correspondences add detail to a complete understanding of both the number and court cards. Generally they show the sphere within which the court card operates and what emerges or results from their acting in the world. For instance, the Queen of Swords operates within the sphere of "Sorrow" (the sephirah Binah, called Understanding). She "understands" being stabbed in the heart as depicted in the Three of Swords. Based on this we might characterize her as "Our Lady of Sorrows." The King of Swords (in Chokmah, called Wisdom) is related to the Two of Swords or "Peace Restored," so he brings his "wisdom" to bear on conflicting dualities, thus suspending animosities. He could be named a "Peacekeeper" with the idea that his force of will and power imposes and maintains that peace.

Pair each of the court cards with the corresponding number card derived from its Tree of Life placement (twos for kings, threes for queens, sixes for princes, and tens for princesses), and determine how the number and court cards might relate to each other. Does their interrelationship suggest an appropriate name for the court card?

The qabalistic correspondences for the court cards, although expressed in terms of the sephiroth and the Tetragrammaton, embody a basic quaternity of four elements. The king and queen are the primordial elements of energetic fire and receptive water, and their offspring are prince and princess, mental air and generative earth.

The key court card correspondences, organized by rank, are shown in the chart on the facing page. You will also find a summary of the Golden Dawn attributions for all sixteen court cards in appendix A.

NOTE ON CHART AT RIGHT

*   These categories also correspond to the suits / elements in the same order, i.e., wands, cups, swords, pentacles and can be cross-combined with their counterparts to form sixteen categories of rank plus suit.

	King/Knight	Queen	Prince/Emperor	Princess/Empress
Element	Fire	Water	Air	Earth
Tattwa	Tejas: a flame-red triangle	Apas: a silver crescent	Vayu: a sky blue circle	Prithivi: a golden yellow square
Tetragrammaton	Yod: Instigating energy	He: Response to and support of the yod energy	Vau: Working out of the yod energy	He (final): Yod energy materialized
Qabalistic World	Atziluth: World of emanation and divinity	Briah: World of creation and angelic spirits	Yetzirah: World of formation	Assiah: World of action or matter
Sephirah	Chokmah: "Wisdom," the 2nd sephirah. The primal male principle	Binah: "Understanding," the 3rd sephirah. The primal female symbol	Tiphareth: "Beauty," the 6th sephirah. Seat of the human will	Malkuth: "Kingdom," the 10th sephirah. Realm of the immanent *shekhinah*
Description	Mounted on steeds	Seated on thrones	Borne on chariots	Standing firmly alone
Effects	Commencement of material forces. Potential power: strong current of activity; swift and violent, soon passes away	Bringer forth of material force. Brooding power: steady, unshaken, enduring (protective)	Realizes the influence of force in king and queen. Power in action: illusionary unless set in motion by father and mother.	Combines the effects of king, queen, and prince. Power of reception and transmission: violent; permanent; material
Golden Dawn Interpretations	Coming or going of a matter, arrival or departure according to the way they face	Actual women connected with the subject	Actual men connected with the subject	Thoughts, feelings, opinions, and ideas in harmony with or opposed to the subject

An Elemental Meditation

Both the ranks of the court cards and their suits, associated with one of the four elements, may at first seem bewildering. What are we to make of a description of the King of Cups as "the fiery part of water," for example? In the *Book of Thoth*, Aleister Crowley lists natural phenomena or environments for each court card (except the princesses) that combine their two elements. For example, the airy part of fire is the sun, the fiery part of air is wind, and the watery part of earth is fields. Each of these has the substance of its primary element (the sun is fire, the wind is air, and the fields are earth), but exhibits some of the qualities of the secondary element (the sun is clear and in the sky, the wind is rapid and energetic, the fields are moist and nurturing of life). Think up you own such natural phenomena for all sixteen combinations (found in appendix C), and write them down. (You don't need to match Crowley's selections.)

Now choose one court card, perhaps one that is especially challenging for you to work with and interpret. What natural phenomenon or environment have you assigned to it?

Now relax and prepare for meditation by focusing on your breath, centering, and closing your eyes. Imagine yourself immersed in the phenomenon or environment of the card. How does this place affect your senses? Is your vision clear or obscured? What do you hear? What do you feel on your skin (heat, cold, wetness)? Are there odors or tastes that you are aware of? Could you live here?

Now allow some portion of this place to take on human form, without losing its elemental qualities. (A face might take shape in the sun, for example, or a wind coalesce into a vortex with twirling limbs.) This elemental creature rules the natural forces you are immersed in. Become aware of its power and authority, here, in its own domain.

Allow the elemental being to react to you. Are you welcomed? What does it communicate to you? What can you learn from it?

Thank the elemental being and find your way back to a more familiar environment. If you are aloft, settle down to earth, if you are underwater, swim to shore. Bring your consciousness back into your physical body. When you feel comfortable, open your eyes and record your thoughts in your journal.

Tattwas

Tattwas (also spelled *tattvas*) are described in a book about Hindu Tantrism called *Nature's Finer Forces* by the theosophist Rama Prasad.[6] Tattwas consist of twenty-five geometric symbols painted on cards. Golden Dawn magicians use them as a focus in open-eyed trance visioning where they become gateways to specific territories in the astral world. Each tattwa is a combination of two out of five basic shapes. Associated with the four elements plus ether, a red triangle is *tejas* or fire, a golden square is *prithivi* or earth, a silver crescent is *apas* or water, a blue circle is *vayu* or air, and an indigo egg is *akasha* or spirit. When two of them are combined, a smaller symbol is superimposed on a larger one. Prithivi of vayu, the earthy part of air, is a golden square superimposed on a larger blue circle. By not using *akasha*, the fifth element, we have four times four tattwas or sixteen combined geometric symbols.

Tattwas were often placed against a background of their complementary color, so that if you stared at it for several minutes and then closed your eyes the image would appear behind your eyelids with the colors switched. In practice, this switch has the effect of throwing you into or even through the image. In a sense you enter into the astral environment of the court card, which you can then explore, bringing back new information and understandings about how the energy of the card functions. The natural phenomena or environments discussed in the previous exercise could thus be explored through a kind of literal astral projection.[7]

Elemental Dignities

One of the most interesting ways to appreciate how the metaphysical energies of the court cards interact with each other, or to evaluate the relative strength or weakness of court cards in a spread, is by using elemental dignities (EDs). You use EDs to examine cards in pairs and triads to determine which suit elements dignify or strength each other (deemed "friendly") and which weaken each other (deemed "contrary"). S. MacGregor Mathers, a founding member of the Hermetic Order of the Golden Dawn, was the first to describe this method of interpreting card combinations or interactions in a document known as *Book T*.[8]

The EDs of the court cards suggest inner, psychological states that are often deeply meaningful. As the suits become less friendly toward each other, they tend to become more paradoxical and stress-creating in one's life. This is because when contrary elements try to operate at the same time, we find contradictory behavior—one part of you wants or does one thing and another part wants or does something quite different.

The basic concept is quite simple. All quotations come from the original text of *Book T*.

Same Suit/Element

- Wands/Wands (Fire/Fire)
- Swords/Swords (Air/Air)
- Cups/Cups (Water/Water)
- Pentacles/Pentacles (Earth/Earth)

When the suits/elements are the same, they are "very strong for either good or evil, according to their nature."

Such pairs tend to highlight, accentuate, emphasize, and give prominence to the cards represented (whether for good or ill). Their energies are synthesized or synchronized. They may be united in action, however, they don't challenge us. There is little external interference, but also little compromise or ability to adjust.

Same Polarity

- Wands/Swords (Fire/Air)
- Cups/Pentacles (Water/Earth)

When the suits/elements are both masculine (yang or positive) or feminine (yin or negative), they are "moderately strong" because they are "friendly to each other."

Such pairs are complementary and compatible. They easily coexist, tending toward compromise, balance, and moderation. They encourage us to seek information and knowledge through communication with, or observation of, the other. At worst, we might deny one in favor of the other. Success comes through balancing these polarized urges and by integrating their commonalities.

Complements

- Swords/Cups (Air/Water)
- Wands/Pentacles (Fire/Earth)

When the suits and elements complement each other, they are "somewhat friendly."

These cards are not totally comfortable with each other. They tend toward excessiveness or inhibition, disorganization or friction. Wands and pentacles can give us intense, sensory desire; swords and cups can be emotionally willful. Both need to control creative power through discrimination. Each tends to receive, stabilize, internalize, secure, or attract the other. They may also act as corrective and therapeutic forces on each other.

Contraries

- Wands/Cups (Fire/Water)
- Swords/Pentacles (Air/Earth)

When the cards are of "contrary elements" they tend to "weaken each other greatly for good or evil, and neutralize their force."

These cards are incompatible and antagonistic, representing conflicts of interest that can lead to stalemate, blocks, or suppression and inhibition of energies. These cards can neutralize each other, allowing a third element to operate more independently. At their worst, the elements work at cross-purposes, producing fear or frustration and a sense of crisis. They expose root vulnerabilities and weak points in the other—revealing insecurities, and uncertainty. Consider what defense mechanisms and mistrust each brings up in the other. Determine what guilt, inadequacy, or fears they engender or assume. On the other hand, each can spur the other to action and provide the energy needed to achieve the seemingly impossible. They force us to grow. Understanding may not be possible but compassionate concern and acceptance may be. Each must learn self-reliance and how to maintain internal as well as external boundaries. Conscious adjustments and modifications are necessary. Finally, we must be willing to let go of untenable situations since holding on can block energy that is needed for moving on elsewhere.

Elemental Dignities in Triads

In triads, the central card is considered the most important with the flanking cards modifying it. Among three cards, "if the contrary element is only in one flanking card, then the other becomes a connecting card so that the first is not weakened, but is modified and therefore fairly strong. If the main card is cups and the flanking cards are wands, then the person may be lacking the qualities shown by the wands cards. If a card passes between two which are naturally contrary, it is not affected by either much, as they weaken each other."

Examples

Suppose a young man, Brad, has started taking voice lessons. He is excited and dedicated to exploring his new skills, but is having problems satisfying his voice teacher.

In a reading, the Page of Pentacles comes up in a position that clearly shows that this is himself with his newfound interest. He recognizes his voice teacher in the Knight of Swords. When asked how this card is like his teacher, he describes him as pushy and critical—always looking for flaws. "My teacher takes all the joy out of it," says Brad. Earth and air are contraries. The knight of Swords would see the Page of Pentacles as naïve, slow, probably not paying attention to the right things, and maybe getting in the way of the teacher's own direction. He would tell the page to "sharpen up" or get out. The Page of Pentacles would see the knight as not stopping to smell the roses, and as perceiving singing as a battle and not as a wondrous experience. If their roles had been switched and the page had been the teacher, he would have focused on the basics, on getting one thing done well before moving on to another, and on savoring or studying the work. The knight as student, would have been anxious to "get somewhere" with his training, rushing to conquer new skills before he had even appreciated the old ones. In Brad's case, unless there were extenuating circumstances, he might do well to find a more compatible teacher. However, we should be aware that sometimes a teacher with an opposing style may be just what a student needs to learn another kind of lesson.

Examine the other cards in the reading, and remember that it is better to give the information to the querent so that the querent can make up his or her own mind. How could this teacher and student agree to disagree and yet still find some way of working with each other? Once Brad has considered this he can decide if it is worth it.

If you have a triad of three court cards (or of any cards with elemental characteristics) and, say, the central one is the Page of Cups, and the Queen of Wands is on one side and the complementary Queen of Pentacles is on the other, then the Page of Cups is affected by both queens (like two mothers) through the mediation of the Queen of Pentacles, which is of the same polarity as cups. If the cards on either side are the contrary Queen of Pentacles and Queen of Swords then, traditionally, their effects cancel each other out. If the flanking cards are the Queen and King of Wands, which are both contrary to cups, then it shows the page is antagonistic to and lacking of their fiery influence.

The Golden Dawn Astrological Correspondences

The Golden Dawn used three interlocking systems for assigning astrological meanings to the cards of the Tarot: one for the major arcana, one for the number cards, and one for the court cards. Although these assignments all stand on their own separately, it is fascinating and informative to explore the connections among them.

In the Qabalist work, *Sepher Yetzirah* (translated from Hebrew sources by Golden Dawn cofounder William Wescott), the Hebrew letters were associated with the signs of the zodiac, the planets, and the elements. These associations have been transferred to the major arcana. Beginning with Aries (as the Emperor), the signs of the zodiac appear in order, except when they skip over cards that are assigned to planets.[9]

The prince, queen, and king of the four suits are associated with the twelve signs of the zodiac: queens are cardinal (Aries, Cancer, Libra, Capricorn), kings (Thoth knight) are mutable (Gemini, Virgo, Sagittarius, Pisces), and princes are fixed (Taurus, Leo, Scorpio, Aquarius). If you are working with a standard deck and traditional interpretations, you may find that kings work better as fixed signs, and traditional knights as mutable signs.

The Golden Dawn wanted to emphasize that people don't manifest as pure elements, so these cards function as mediators or links between the elements. Each court card presides over one-third of one sign and element, and two-thirds of the sequentially following sign and element. These "thirds" are known as *decans* or *decanates*. If you take the twelve signs of the zodiac and divide each in three segments of ten degrees each, the result is thirty-six decans. The sun takes about ten days to travel through a decan. The concept was first developed in Egypt, was popular during the Renaissance, and is still used in astrology today. The Queen of Wands, for example, rules from twenty degrees of Pisces to twenty degrees of Aries, or one-third of the former sign and two-thirds of the latter. She presides over a period from March 11 to April 10. March 11 through 20 are the last ten days of Pisces, and March 21 through April 10 are the first twenty days of Aries. If you like the idea of choosing a significator astrologically, this makes an interesting alternative to the one-sign-per-card approach. (Dates for each court card are given in appendix C.)

The Golden Dawn also assigned each number card (excluding the aces) to one of the thirty-six decans. They began with the Two of Wands in the first decan of Aries, then the three in the second, and so on. Each decan is ruled by a planet, although there are several different orderings. The Golden Dawn used what is called the Chaldean order of the planets, which reflects their speed of movement: Saturn, Jupiter, Mars, Sun, Venus, Mercury, Moon (fastest to slowest). This is the same order that the planets appear on the Tree of Life. The decans begin and end with Mars so, for example, Mars, Sun, and Venus are in Aries, continuing with Mercury, Moon, Saturn in Taurus, and so on until they end with Mars in Pisces.

Cards numbered two, three, and four are associated with the cardinal sign of their element, for instance, the Two of Wands goes with the first decan of cardinal fire or Aries. The five, six, and seven go with the fixed sign of their element. The eight, nine, and ten go with the mutable sign of their element. Another way to look at it is that the numerical sequence continues sequentially through the signs of the zodiac—two, three, four, five, six . . . (Aries, Taurus, etc.) but when a new sign is entered (switching from cardinal to fixed to mutable) the suit changes to correspond with the element of the new sign. Thus the last decan in Aries is given to the Four of Wands, but is followed by the Five of Pentacles for the first decan of Taurus. A summary of all these astrological assignments is presented in the chart on the facing page.

Zodiac Sign: element (Major Arcana Card)	Court Card	Astrological Decans (Number Card)
(Last decan of Pisces)	Queen	Mars in Pisces (10 of Cups)
Aries:	of Wands	Mars in Aries (2 of Wands)
cardinal fire		Sun in Aries (3 of Wands)
(The Emperor)	Prince	Venus in Aries (4 of Wands)
Taurus:	of Pentacles	Mercury in Taurus (5 of Pentacles)
fixed earth		Moon in Taurus (6 of Pentacles)
(The Hierophant)	King	Saturn in Taurus (7 of Pentacles)
Gemini:	of Swords	Jupiter in Gemini (8 of Swords)
mutable air		Mars in Gemini (9 of Swords)
(The Lovers)	Queen	Sun in Gemini (10 of Swords)
Cancer:	of Cups	Venus in Cancer (2 of Cups)
cardinal water		Mercury in Cancer (3 of Cups)
(The Chariot)	Prince	Moon in Cancer (4 of Cups)
Leo:	of Wands	Saturn in Leo (5 of Wands)
fixed fire		Jupiter in Leo (6 of Wands)
(Strength)	King	Mars in Leo (7 of Wands)
Virgo:	of Pentacles	Sun in Virgo (8 of Pentacles)
mutable earth		Venus in Virgo (9 of Pentacles)
(The Hermit)	Queen	Mercury in Virgo (10 of Pentacles)
Libra:	of Swords	Moon in Libra (2 of Swords)
cardinal air		Saturn in Libra (3 of Swords)
(Justice)	Prince	Jupiter in Libra (4 of Swords)
Scorpio:	of Cups	Mars in Scorpio (5 of Cups)
fixed water		Sun in Scorpio (6 of Cups)
(Death)	King	Venus in Scorpio (7 of Cups)
Sagittarius:	of Wands	Mercury in Sagittarius (8 of Wands)
mutable fire		Moon in Sagittarius (9 of Wands)
(Temperance)	Queen	Saturn in Sagittarius (10 of Wands)
Capricorn:	of Pentacles	Jupiter in Capricorn (2 of Pentacles)
cardinal earth		Mars in Capricorn (3 of Pentacles)
(The Devil)	Prince	Sun in Capricorn (4 of Pentacles)
Aquarius:	of Swords	Venus in Aquarius (5 of Swords)
fixed air		Mercury in Aquarius (6 of Swords)
(The Star)	King	Moon in Aquarius (7 of Swords)
Pisces:	of Cups	Saturn in Pisces (8 of Cups)
mutable water		Jupiter in Pisces (9 of Cups)
(The Moon)		Mars in Pisces (10 of Cups)

Reading across the chart, one finds three number cards and two major arcana cards associated with each court card. These associated cards can enrich the meaning of the court card by showing what issues (major arcana) and functions and qualities (number cards) the figure on the card is inclined to be involved with. In a reading, these associations can heighten your awareness of connections between different cards in the spread.

For example, let's see what those cards say about the King/Knight of Swords (the figure on horseback). He has characteristics of the first two decans of the mutable air sign, Gemini, and the last decan of the preceding fixed earth sign, Taurus. These correspond with the number cards: Seven of Pentacles (success unfulfilled), Eight of Swords (shortened force), and Nine of Swords (despair and cruelty), which form a three-card reading describing how the king functions. Note: Golden Dawn card interpretations have been used in the illustrations on the facing page.

These cards portray the horseman of swords as a person who loses what he tries to cultivate; early promise goes unfulfilled (Seven of Pentacles). This could be because he tends to apply too much force to small things. He holds to the letter of the law rather than the greater principles behind it; his attention to detail can get him tied up in knots (Eight of Swords). The result is agony of mind. He inflicts unnecessary suffering and misery on himself and others since his conscience and sense of duty require the impossible (Nine of Swords).

Astrologically speaking, this King/Knight of Swords has the qualities of Saturn in Taurus, Jupiter in Gemini, and Mars in Gemini. Saturn in Taurus suggests that the King of Swords has characteristics we might not otherwise have seen. Saturn in an earth sign gives persistence and stamina (or obstinacy and doggedness) similar to the Hierophant, and can make this king jealous and possessive—like the patriarchs of the Old Testament. He has to discover what he really values. Discipline and hard work are necessary to give him the security he needs, but his Gemini attributes will work counter to this. Jupiter in Gemini is detrimental to the king, resulting in scattered or overly expansive thinking and rashness. He's mentally restless and changeable with a need to travel. This is the intellectual side of the religious impulse and, at its best, can lend itself to diplomacy. Mars in Gemini (Nine of Swords) is

The King of Swords and three corresponding cards from
The Golden Dawn Magical Tarot

intellectually aggressive. It increases the king's excitability and irritability, making him argumentative, witty, and sarcastic. He defends his ideas, but his efforts may be intermittent, which could create unbearable tension with the Saturn in Taurus part of himself. These attributes emphasize the reckless abandon and arbitrariness of Cupid's arrows in the corresponding Lovers card, and the vacillation of the Lover in the Marseilles-style decks, where he is unable to decide between two women.

This combination seems to work best in a commercial capacity where one has to "sell" an idea he or she deeply believes in. It can also make for a good investigative journalist. It unfortunately also resembles inquisitors and defenders of the faith who seek to cut out all vestiges of heresy and secure the supremacy of their own beliefs. Consider whether such qualities are more like the King or Knight in your own deck.

A Numerical Analysis of the Court Cards

The Tarot cards can be seen as a model of coming to "know ourselves"— an admonition written on the gate of the Oracle at Delphi. Since numbers so often form the inner structure of the Tarot, we can turn to them in our attempt to better understand the court cards. There are no individual numbers associated with the court cards, but there are a total of sixteen of them. We shall see if a significance can be found for this.

The sixteenth major arcana card is the Tower, which is also known as the House of God, Tower of Destruction, and the Great Liberator. This is the card that liberates us from the structures and forms that keep us from perceiving our true selves. In it, the lightning bolt of truth destroys all false boundaries and beliefs. And the structures, boundaries, and beliefs that are destroyed in this card are, of course, the roles that each of us play in our daily lives. These roles are the masks we hide behind. They are the fences and walls we build to keep us, and others, from the realization of who we really are. They form our "identity," or that which makes us different from others. These enclosing walls protect us from the unknown; thus we nest down in a structure of false security, false because these personality structures—ones like those you've listed earlier in this book—are not who you really are. You are not the walls around you, but rather the multiform spirit that resides within.

Thus, the Tower exemplifies the idea that the court cards reflect the personality roles we play, the masks we hide behind, and the towering forms we've crystalized into, which must ultimately be destroyed if we are to awaken to who we really are. The Tower stresses the impermanence of worldly position and rank and the false sense of importance and pride of achievement in which we cloak ourselves. We are truly liberated when we have no more roles to play; when our infinite possibilities are no longer limited.

Now, if we add one plus six, we get seven, and perhaps the seventh trump card can tell us something more about the essential nature of these sixteen court cards.

Seven is the number of the Chariot, also known as Victory or Mastery. The vehicle pictured on the card represents our own personal temple from which our power flows into our daily experience. A work on Tarot called *Jewels of the Wise* explains how we have built vehicles or enclosures to imprison our inner subconscious self. These are enclosures within which we cultivate who we are and develop our various masteries in our daily life.[10]

The lunar masks on the charioteer's shoulders and the duality and mixed characteristics of the sphinxes show that we wear the masks to pose our own riddle to the sphinx's question, "Who am I?" The zodiacal belt suggests that we wear these masks of personality as long as time and space bind us.

Our individual vehicle is the enclosure in which we cultivate ourselves. The court cards are therefore the ways in which we gain mastery and perfect ourselves. They are the developmental steps we take to discover our own identity. Like the Chariot, the court cards show us how to develop control over our physical environment, how to harness our personal resources toward a purpose, and how to use our skills and abilities to move instinctively through the challenges presented in the minor arcana number cards. The court cards depict us, the querents, on a journey of self-development. As the Bhagavad Gita says, "The Self is the rider in the chariot of the body, of which the senses are horses and the mind the reins." We are the self within an ever-changing vehicle consisting of social and developmental roles.

And, thus, we see how we develop and perfect our personality structure, and then, as in the Tower, go through a process of breaking down all that is false in that structure, only to slowly build it up again. We may discover our restructured personalities are still not who we really are. And so we continue until we have burned away all the forms that keep us from mirroring truth and perfection. Then, we too can see our reflection in the Holy Grail as pictured in the Thoth Chariot card.

Finally, let's look at the sixteen court cards again, and at the number sixteen, specifically, the one and the six. Translated into major arcana cards, these are the Magician and the Lovers. This seems appropriate because, in interpretation, the court cards work in two core ways:

1. As the Magician indicates, these cards always represent some aspect of the person the reading is about: old numero uno, "number one," me, myself, and I.

2. As the Lovers card shows, the court cards also refer to someone you are in relationship with. In the Lovers card, a mirroring is taking place between the inner and outer self. The conscious mind looks to the subconscious mind, which is focused on the higher self for guidance. We can look at the people we draw into our lives as mirrors of our own inner processes—sometimes our shadowy negative self-images, and other times those highest qualities we are blind to in ourselves.[11]

So when the court cards appear in a spread, it is important to read them from both points of view: as an aspect of yourself, and in the role of others teaching you about yourself.

And, of course, as we saw, one plus six add up to seven, and so we are back to the Chariot: we develop self-mastery through our interactions with others, by seeing the different aspects of ourselves reflected in some way by everyone we come in contact with. (See illustration on facing page.)

Values Exercise

Metaphysical systems can sometimes seem arcane and baroque, clothed as they often are in foreign or antiquated language and laden with complex relationships that may seem to demand years of memorization to master.

A value is something of fundamental importance, a thing that feels like an end in itself. Values can usually be expressed in a single word or a short

*Four major arcana numerogically related to the court cards
from the* Universal Waite Tarot

phrase. When we ask ourselves serious questions about what path our lives should take, or how best to live in this world, it is our values that come into play and shape our answers. Values are different from goals. Making money, for example, is a common goal. Many people pursue it. But why? Most often, the reasons have to do with fundamental needs for things like security, respect, health, and the like. These are the values that drive many of us to make money. If something is clearly a means to an end, it is not a value.

Identify important values in your life, such as friendship, health, and so on. Write each on a separate index card or piece of paper. If you feel artistic, you can illustrate each one with a suitable symbol, color, or drawing. Be open to more global values, such as those behind political or environmental goals, or religious or spiritual commitments, but be honest with yourself. Don't affirm something as a value just because you think you ought to. Attend to what really matters to you. If necessary, take a hard look at how you actually spend your time and energy, and what really gives you satisfaction. Identify as many values as you can without forcing it. A dozen or so is a good number for this exercise, but fewer or more are okay.

Now take the index cards and play with the arrangement of them. You might start by arranging them in a line, ordered by importance, perhaps, or from personal to communal, or some other criteria. Then try being more creative, making two-dimensional patterns. Use your intuition to place each value where it seems to fit best in relation to the others.

The result is a diagram of your personal value system. It's a picture of your world, not in terms of physical objects or geography or chronology, but in terms of what matters to you and motivates you.

Now go through your Tarot deck and find the card that best symbolizes each of your values. Some may be easy (if one of your values is "justice," for example); others will be more challenging. Did you select any court cards? Which ones? Record the pattern you created in your journal, and make a note of any thought that occur to you as you look at your personal value map.

ENDNOTES

1 For an excellent historical overview of the contemporary pagan movement and its sources, see *The Triumph of the Moon: A History of Modern Pagan Witchcraft* by Ronald Hutton.

2 *Songs for the Journey Home*, a Tarot deck created by Catherine Cook and Dwariko von Sommaruga.

3 See *The Pythagorean Tarot* by John Opsopaus (deck illustrations by Rho).

4 See *Tarot of Ceremonial Magick* by Lon Milo DuQuette. See also *Book T*.

5 The original Golden Dawn text used a slightly different system for aligning court cards with sephiroth. Chokmah and the four deuces are the Powers of the King and Queen. Binah and the threes represent the Prince and Princess as "the realization of action owing to the Prince being produced" (*Book T*).

6 For more information on tattwas, see Israel Regardie's *Complete Golden Dawn System of Magic* or, for a modern exploration with cards included, *Magicial Tattwa Cards: A Complete System for Self-Development* by Dr. Jonn Mumford.

7 Some people believe that the forceful physiological effects that result from using complementary colors can be dangerous to the psyche. Dr. Mumford's book (mentioned above) offers sound and sensible guidance.

8 The text of *Book T* is in Robert Wang's *An Introduction to the Golden Dawn Tarot* and in Israel Regardie's *The Complete Golden Dawn System of Magic*.

9 Users of the Thoth deck should note that Aleister Crowley exchanged Hebrew letter assignments, and hence the astrological correspondences, for the Emperor and Star cards.

10 The Holy Order of Mans, *Jewels of the Wise*, pp. 73–79.

11 This concept was pointed out by Paul Foster Case in his book *The Tarot: A Key to the Wisdom of the Ages*.

CHAPTER SEVEN

ℬringing It All Together

In the first six chapters of this book, we looked at the court cards from many different angles. If you've been trying out the exercises and spreads, your journal probably has quite a few entries and notes for each of the court cards in your deck. And if you've been working with Tarot for a while before starting this book, you probably have more bits and pieces of insight and wisdom tucked away in notebooks or in your head. It may feel a bit like a pack rat's attic—lots of good ideas lying around somewhere, but never the right one nearby when you need it! This chapter is intended to help you put your personal court "in order" so you can read court cards with more confidence and flexibility.

Just for Fun

Take all sixteen court cards right-side up, shuffle them, and lay them out in a line from your personal favorite (the card you like the most) to your least favorite. If you have trouble determining the line-up, look at cards in pairs and decide which you like more until you find the right spot. By the time you get to the last card you should have established a most-to-least-favored sequence—then, if necessary, refine it. Remember, this is just for fun, so you can do anything you like. Write down the line-up and date it so when you do it again someday you can compare how your perceptions have changed.

Now, look for patterns, does one rank or suit fall entirely in the first or last half? Are there any surprises? Can you find natural pairings (couples) or groups? Do they seem to tell a story? Describe the qualities of your most favorite and least favorite cards. Put them together in a pair: what makes them so different? Make up a relationship between the two of them. What "bright shadow" qualities does your most favorite card have? What "dark shadow" qualities does your least favorite card have? Where does your significator fall? What cards are it next to and what's their story? Where is your nemesis card? What is its story in the line-up? What is the central pair or grouping? Referring back to other exercises—where do friends-and-family cards fall?

For instance, Mary had the Queen of Swords and King of Cups as most and least favorite, respectively. When paired, the king looked at the queen as if expecting the sword to fall on him at any moment. It's as if the queen were asking too much of him so that he just wanted to shrink away. Three of the pages were in the middle—along with the nurturing Queen of Pentacles who seemed to be fondly watching their play. It was as if they were being hidden or protected from danger. When comparing with a line-up done five years previously, Mary discovered that her top three favorites were the same, although in different order, and that three out of four of the last cards were the same. The pages had moved the most (they moved down the line), and she had switched the positions of two kings. The pages troubled her as she realized she had locked away much of her sense of play in an attempt to focus on work.

The Tarot School Court Card Personality Array

Wald and Ruth Ann Amberstone of the Tarot School in New York teach a technique they call the Court Card Personality Array. The entire process requires in-depth training, but they've given permission for one step to be explained here in a very simplified format.

Determine your favorite suit. Take the court cards from just that one suit and place them in a row from your personal favorite (on the left) to least favorite (on far right). Once you've done this, use the following concepts to gain insight.

- Your most favorite court card (in that suit) shows your strengths, talents, and dominant mode in the qualities connected with that suit. It indicates natural affinities and positive responses, and what you most want to be like.

- Your second favorite card shows a more intimate, less visible aspect of your personality, that either augments and supports, or alternates with, the dominant mode in that suit. This is your alter ego.

- Your third favorite card shows what motivates you: issues that challenge or frustrate you in that suit. You may be working on issues here, and must pay attention to these qualities.

- Your least favorite card is most difficult for you to access. It is what you like least and perhaps even dislike. Liked least, it is usually ignored. Disliked, its qualities can become an obsession. It can be disowned and rejected or even projected outward as the enemy. The meanings usually associated with reversed court cards might be applied here.

In interpreting the Court Card Personality Array, it is sometimes helpful to look at the first two cards as a pair, and then the second two cards as a pair.

For instance, Jana chose the suit of pentacles (security, facts, body, self-worth) and led with the page and followed by the king. She saw her student-self, who is open, questioning, amazed by life, alternating with a certain arrogant sense of competence and mastery. She wanted to seem open, flexible, and innocent, but underneath she knew exactly what she valued and believed (the king). Her third card was the Queen of Pentacles. In the material-world sphere, Jana was motivated by riches and luxury, and needed to pay attention to issues of prosperity and security. Being the last card and least liked, the knight's steady perseverance was most difficult for her to access. She felt obsessed by her desire to avoid boredom and the stubborn attitudes she believed to be her enemy.

If you wish, do this with all four suits. The cards in your least favorite suit will be more difficult for you to access than the cards in your favorite suit. Consider how you might be projecting their qualities onto others.

Thinking about Keywords

Although some readers regard keywords as a bit trite—the Tarot equivalents of "soundbites" on the nightly news—the process of developing your own keywords for each card can be enormously valuable. Can you describe yourself in ten words? The result is certain to be incomplete, but the process of making the attempt can be stimulating, rewarding, and probing. In this book, we assume that, although your interpretations of the court cards will be informed by Tarot tradition, there will also be a personal dimension involved: you have a unique relationship with each card, and that relationship is a strength to be drawn on when reading the Tarot for yourself and others.

If you have a collection of notes for each court card, review them and mark a few entries that seem especially profound. Perhaps something struck you while doing an exercise, or you had an insight into the nature of the card from a special reading. If you haven't been journaling (like one of the authors, who has a fine collection of aborted journals on his shelf), you can still write down a few of your strongest associations for each court card.

After you've made note of your strongest impressions for each card, you may notice that you have a preference for one style of interpretation. Perhaps most of your phrases are psychological, or have to do with astrology or Qabalah, or maybe they are very concrete attributes: appearance, profession, relationship. Make a second pass through the court, trying to fill in modes of interpretation you've neglected. If, for example, you're a personality aficionado, add in some concrete, physical characteristics and some metaphysical dimensions.

Now comes the hard part. Look at the court cards as a group and ask yourself two questions:

- Is the difference between some cards blurred, so that they seem to signify practically the same thing? (For example, do you regard both the Page of Cups and the Page of Pentacles as dreamy youths, receptive and passive children waiting for life to happen to them?)

- Do the sixteen court cards really cover the full range of human personas, or are there conspicuous gaps? (For example, are there none of the court cards that you see as happy, or sentimental, or critical?)

If two cards seem very similar, you need to work on the contrasts between them. Perhaps that Page of Cups is poetic, musical, and artistic, while the Page of Pentacles is practical, loyal, and industrious. Find the qualities that help separate the cards from each other and add those to your potential keywords.

The second question can be challenging. It might not be obvious what has been left out. It may be helpful to think of personal situations you have been involved with in recent years (and also situations your friends have been involved with), and jot down the "key players" as well as their distinguishing traits are. Also, attend to domains of life that may not be prominent in your own reality. You may not have children, but your keywords still need to capture parenting issues. Or you may be very focused on your own spiritual path, but your keywords still need to capture work, relationships, and other practical realities. If you find domains of the human condition that you've neglected, ask yourself which court cards in your deck would best capture those concepts.

Now you are ready to craft your own personal set of keywords for each card. The exact form of the keywords is, of course, up to you. However, it is nice to use some concrete nouns that you associate with people and connect those nouns with adjectives to make the keywords richer. This emphasizes that the court cards are people, while still allowing abstract and archetypal qualities to enter in.

For example, you may have noted the following as key concepts for the King of Cups: nurturing, sentimental, lord of emotions, fire of water, Cancer, grandpa, musician, lost opportunities, irrationality. These ideas might be combined into adjective/noun pairs as follows: a sentimental musician, a nurturing grandfather, an irrational caretaker, a nostalgic lord.

Notice how the nouns are all "person" words, reminding us that the court cards can always refer to ourselves or others, while the adjectives suggest some of the more abstract energies behind the card. Try this adjective/noun pattern to develop a few phrases for each court card, but feel free to add words or phrases of a different pattern as well. Sometimes, in looking over your keywords, an abstract noun may come to mind: integrity, perversity, industriousness. These one-word syntheses are quite valuable and should be included. Don't worry if the phrases at this point seem a little redundant or uninspired; you'll have opportunity to perfect them later.

In doing this process, you may find that some of the cards don't suggest much to you at all. When you discover this kind of impasse, a good approach is to do an "enter the card" meditation, and spend some quality time with this particular personality.

It is valuable at this point to begin to view the cards as a system, rather than just as individual personages. From the other exercises, you'll be getting a feel for what the cards of each suit and each rank have in common, in terms of personalities, roles, professions, and values. See if you can capture those common threads in a few keywords. Recall that each suit may represent a particular area of life, and each rank a different style of functioning in that area. So, for example, if your deck seems to confirm the conventional wisdom linking the suit of cups with matters of the heart, and linking knights with dynamic, outward energy, then the Knight of Cups would signify someone with a dynamic heart: a daring lover, seducer, or emotionally expressive person. Don't be concerned, however, if your impressions of the court cards in your deck do not seem in tune with conventional wisdom. Follow the lead of the cards themselves, but keep in mind the following guidelines:

- Each suit and each rank should be distinct from the others; try not to have two or more that cover nearly the same ground. You may need to accentuate contrasts and deemphasize similarities to bring this into focus.

- The four suits together should come as close as possible to covering all aspects of life, and the four ranks together should pretty much span the different approaches people use in dealing with them. If your initial impressions were very concrete and specific, you may need to generalize them some and look for appropriate abstractions.

- Make sure you can connect your suit keywords with the symbols themselves in some way. If you decide that swords are about devotion, generosity, and helpfulness (which is not inconceivable, depending on your personal impressions of the court card figures), you will need to give some account of how swords might symbolize these qualities rather than more traditional ones, such as conflict or bravery.

Now make another pass through the court cards, looking at the individual card, the suit keywords, and the rank keywords. Search your mind for words or images that integrate these three aspects of the card. Three to six simple phrases (they might be just single words) for each card is a good number to aim for. Try to find at least one general verbal recipe for interpreting the card (such as: "a leader in household matters") and at least one specific, vivid image ("a victim of unrequited love"). If you don't achieve literary brilliance with every phrase you produce, don't worry; most of the gain comes from making the effort. Sometimes the right words will spring to mind days or weeks after going through the exercise.

After going through all the cards, make a final pass through to make sure you're satisfied with the result. Ask questions like:

- Do the keywords mesh comfortably with the images?
- Are there cards whose keywords are too similar, leaving them both indistinct?
- Do the keywords adequately cover the range of human types and behaviors, or are there blind spots in the system?
- Do these words conjure up strong impressions in my mind, or will they still leave me groping for ideas during a reading?

Successfully completing this exercise gives one the foundation of mastery over the court cards in the deck, allowing you to read them with confidence. Card interpretations, though, are never truly finalized. They continue to grow and change as you watch how the cards work in readings, and as you yourself grow and learn. You may want to keep your keywords in your journal as a living document, which you can add to and update as you work with the cards over time.

EXAMPLE

The keywords that follow were developed specifically for the Swiss *1JJ* deck using the methods outlined above. They won't work as well for other decks but serve as a good example of developing your own keyword system. Notice how they include both single words and phrases, and both concrete and abstract ideas. In going through the process, the following central themes were identified for the suits and ranks of this particular deck. Note how these themes are reflected in the individual card keywords.

Suits	Ranks
• batons: directness	• kings: presence
• cups: imagination	• queens: relationship
• swords: autonomy	• knights: action
• coins: duty	• pages: service

BATONS

King of Batons: a powerful presence, an authority figure; mastery; a patriarch; taking charge without reservation or ambivalence.

Queen of Batons: an honest, outgoing person, assertive in relationships; social confidence.

Knight of Batons: a strong, physically active person; action uncomplicated by thoughts; an athlete; roughness; a bully.

Page of Batons: a sensitive dreamer; a sympathetic friend; open creativity; ease, conviviality; pleasantness.

CUPS

King of Cups: an imaginative eccentric; a retired virtuoso; an absent-minded professor; nostalgia; regret.

Queen of Cups: a busybody; a talkative nurse or cook; a psychic; a person of strong, sudden moods.

Knight of Cups: a flamboyant artist; acting out fantasies; playing a part with style; sensuality; fashion.

Page of Cups: a brooding, moody person; a sensitive person trapped in a servile role; wounded dreams.

SWORDS

King of Swords: a self-reliant leader; mental power; a scientist; a master strategist; final decisions.

Queen of Swords: an entrepreneur; a manipulator; using others to further one's goals; working discretely for a personally important cause; activism.

Court cards from the Swiss 1JJ *deck*

Knight of Swords: a daring agent of change; enforcer; self-assertion; taking defensive action; being harsh and uncompromising to achieve an end.

Page of Swords: a cold, untrusting person; a strong ego deprived of power; a criminal; anxiety; secret excitements.

COINS

King of Coins: a person of integrity; an ally; competence; aiding others through reputation, influence, or resources.

Queen of Coins: a shy but high-strung person; a sense of obligation to others; retreat from conflict; a sensitive child.

Knight of Coins: a loyal stalwart; dedication to family; acting out one's duty.

Page of Coins: a hard worker; fairness; parenting; pride in a job well done; endurance; remaining focused on one's task.

So Who Is It, Anyway?

We've seen how each court card has a distinct personality, and how they can also represent people who take on certain roles or work in certain professions. And, because each of us has a multifaceted personality and can take on many different roles, a court card can always represent some aspect of oneself.

So how is one to know, when the King of Coins pops up, if he represents the banker to whom you went to ask for a loan or your own capacity to manage practical affairs with competence and success? Or, maybe this card stands for something even more abstract, like spiritual power manifesting through earthly events?

Ultimately, your own reactions to the card must guide you between alternative interpretations. However, here is a checklist of things to look at in deciding how to interpret a court card.

- **The spread position:** Some positions lead naturally to a certain interpretation. If the card shows up in a position that is described as "how you appear to others," for example, then it is natural to see the court card as representing a role you are taking on or a personality trait you are exhibiting. On the other hand, if the position description is "external influences," then the card may very well be someone else, whom you can recognize by personality, role, or perhaps profession.

- **Other cards:** Sometimes the other cards in the spread are telling a clear story, and one interpretation of the court cards makes it fit in better than others do. For example, if most of the cards relate to the querent's rivalry with her siblings, a Knight of Wands might very well represent her brother, rather than some aspect of herself.

- **Nature of the question:** If the question is introspective and psychologically or spiritually focused, it is always helpful to consider court cards as aspects of the querent's personality. With a more nuts-and-bolts, outwardly focused question ("How can I pay my electric bill when my next check comes in three weeks?" or, "How can I deal with my landlord when I know I can't pay my rent this month?"), it may be more productive to see a court card as a particular person in the querent's life.

- **Special associations:** As the reader, do you perceive a special connection between the card and the querent or someone in the querent's life? If the deck uses astrological correspondences prominently, and the card matches the querent's sun sign (or the sign of the querent's partner, say), then consider the person so indicated. The querent's personal sense of identification with the card applies here too, not just formal correspondences. Does the querent have a favorite signficator?

- **Deck designer's intentions:** Some decks are designed with a strongly literal, psychological, or metaphysical approach to the court cards. If the companion book to a deck (and its symbolism) strongly encourages you to view the court cards as the actions of a person or as an event, then it is worthwhile to focus on that type of interpretation, unless there is a clear reason to depart from it.

- **Projected traits:** Don't forget that the phenomenon of projection (discussed in chapter 5) suggests that interpreting the card as an aspect of the querent's personality may always be pertinent, even if there are strong reasons for also seeing the card as another person, an event, or a metaphysical influence.

Reading for Others: A Few Hints

- Ask the querent to simply describe the card (objectively and literally—without interpretation), and then to describe the figure's mood, attitude, and emotions. Note where there are strong similarities or differences between what the querent says and standard interpretations. Pay special attention to any unusual interpretations, especially with reversals, where they will likely be key to why the card is reversed. Note when the querent becomes more animated or intense as an internal recognition has taken place. Ask the querent who is most like this description, or how the querent themselves is like this.

- Unless the position or neighboring cards dictate otherwise, offer the querent a range of keywords and options for what a court card may mean and let the querent tell you which is most accurate—let it be his or her insight! But, at the same time, keep the other options, in the back of your mind. One may come in handy at a later point in the reading. For instance, the querent insists there are no children in his life, but later realizes the Page of Pentacles card might refer to his nephew whom he promised to take to a baseball game. On the other hand, be prepared to let go of such an interpretation if there is really no hint of its relevance for the querent. A king or queen do not always point to parental issues!

- Get specific. Ask the querent to describe how the card is like the person the querent identified. What characteristics does the card have that are like this person? Use the querent's own words whenever possible. If the querent says the Queen of Wands is "not nurturing, but smothering," then see how the word "smothering" fits in the context of the whole reading. Does "smothering" suggest other concepts that might relate by rank or suit? "Smothering" suggests that the fire aspects of this card might be active since a person can smother during a fire, especially if there is a lack of air. Also, the closeness of the word to "mother" suggests how this person might have felt in relation to a fiery mother. But ask if it is so, rather than assume it to be the case.

- When a querent reacts strongly to a card, ask him or her what prompted that reaction. Accept the querent's perception. For instance, if the querent finds the Queen of Cups scary, ask the querent what is scary about her, rather than trying to change the person's mind by insisting that the Queen of Cups is really loving and gentle. You can, however, point out the contrast in perception. As the reader, do this in a positive, exploratory way, so that it does not seem like you're suggesting the the querent is wrong, but rather encouraging the querent's perception as an interesting perspective on the card.

- Accept the querent's evaluation regarding whether a quality or characteristic of a court card is operating for good or ill in his or her life, unless the position meaning specifies otherwise. It is, for example, okay to assume the more negative aspects of the Page of Cups in the spread position of "what is blocking you." But, the same card in the position of "the past" could be operating anywhere along a range from good to bad or happy to sad, etc. To discern the querent's attitude to the Knight of Wands, for instance, you might say, "This card can be fiery. Do you enjoy that fieriness or find it overwhelming?"

- Have the querent act like the court card. Direct the querent in assuming the exact posture and ask what it feels like. Then have the querent talk from that personality.

- Ask the querent to make up what the court cards would say or recommend concerning the situations depicted in other cards in the spread. Let the court cards talk to each other. Opinions and attitudes expressed in such spontaneous dialogs will probably be similar to those expressed by people the querent knows or by different aspects of the self. Comparing responses can point up internal and external conflicts and show where the querent will find support, criticism, or demands.

- Look for similarities between the symbols on, or the keywords for, the court cards and other cards in the spread. Such similarities suggest that the two cards might be related. Strong differences suggest there may be little in common. The pentacle held by the Page of Pentacles sometimes looks like the sun in the Sun card. Where no similarities exist like between the Queen of Cups and the Tower, the Queen of Cups, could be, literally, out of her element—that is, weakened by a lack of water.

- Allow for the ridiculous, unexpected, or purely psychic. One woman received the Knight of Pentacles reversed and the Tarot reader, fixated on the oak leaf on his helmet, went with her intuition and asked what the woman had to do with the Oak King of the Elves. The woman was astounded because this was an important figure in her inner life.

Sample Reading

To understand how court cards can be read in a regular spread, here is an example of a Celtic Cross reading. Hannah is a writer in her late forties. She wanted to know what she most needed to look at concerning the problems she was having writing a nonfiction book on writing. She asked, "What is really the core of the work I am doing? Did I make up this book project simply for the sake of my ego, or is it really something I need to be doing?"

The Tarot reader served primarily to ask Hannah questions about the cards and point out connections among them and their symbols. Most of the descriptions and insights were elicited from Hannah.

Hannah picked the Queen of Cups to signify her identity when she was in the flow of her writing. She felt the only other possibility was the Queen of Wands, but saw her as a little dry. She felt like the Queen of Cups in the posture of her body—looking down into her computer screen or onto paper. She noted the water flowing past her—all around the chair—but her feet were firmly on the rocks. The cup especially interested her.

"I always saw these as little demons and not angels [on the sides of the cup]—so it has this strange sort of demonic, robot effect—but then I look at [the cup's decoration] and see [them as] little angels. There is some kind of weird thing with me and the cup. It's almost like an imaginary friend that is always with me, but it's also closed off, like a great mystery. It should have eyes. It talks to me through my looking into it. That's how I look into things in my writing. If writing reveals life, then that's also, for me, what my writing is. I relate the cliffs in the background to places I've lived—Santa Barbara, Martha's Vineyard. It's another way the card's connected to me."

Since her sun was in Cancer, a water sign, this card was astrologically appropriate, although the reader felt that Hannah was far more practical than she was expressing through her choice.

The cards in the spread (illustrated on opposite page) were:

1. What covers her: Hermit

2. What crosses her: Nine of Wands

3. What is below her: The Sun

4. What is behind her: Page of Pentacles reversed

5. What is above her: Three of Pentacles

6. What is before her: Three of Cups

7. Herself: Magician

8. Her environment: Seven of Swords reversed

9. Her hopes and fears: Empress reversed

10. Her personal energy in the near future: Queen of Pentacles reversed

Hannah saw the first two crossing cards, the Hermit and Nine of Wands, as both being essentially alone. One was older than she and the other younger. She didn't have the muscular strength and stamina of the Nine of Wands but was not ready to "call it quits" like the Hermit. He's accepted everything as finished, deciding not to write the book—but she still wanted to write it. Other differences were that one card was winter and the other spring, and one was night and the other day. She cried as she felt the heart issue emerge as the dilemma about whether she should write the book or not. The Nine of Wands had the strength to write it and the Hermit didn't. She experienced a longing to just accept that it didn't need to be done, but then she felt her ego pushing her to do something. The Hermit was her naturally introverted nature while the Nine of Wands kept pushing her to share her extensive and hard-won experience.

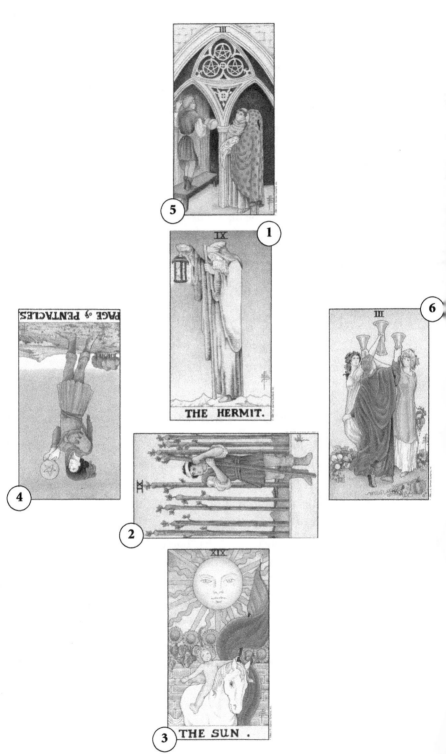

Hannah's Celtic Cross with cards from the Universal Waite Tarot

10 QUEEN of PENTACLES *(reversed)*

9 THE EMPRESS. *(reversed)* III

8 VII *(reversed)*

7 I

THE MAGICIAN.

At the base of the matter, in the root or unconscious, was the Sun card. The Sun at the root of herself was the ego insisting that the book be written. It said, "This is who you are, and this is what you do." But she identified more with the horse in the card's picture since she also has a way of looking down and then up again—mischievously. The horse looked like a playful demon who seemed to say, "I dare you." Hannah couldn't relate to the child on the card at all. The potential to give birth to this "child" project was clearly there, but the energy was deeply buried.

The Page of Pentacles reversed in the past would traditionally point to problems with a child, studies, bad news, or difficulty in childhood. Hannah thought he had goals that were superficial and "not lofty." When upright, he was nice enough, but not a very strong person. When reversed, he lost control of his goal and was scared. Four days before, she had let go of her goals, deciding not to write the book after all—giving it up, yet again. The goals didn't seem worthwhile. Her book had lost its value. This abandonment reminded her of when, sitting on a porch as a child, she decided she was not able to draw or paint and then gave it up. His pentacle was like a miniature sun. The horse on the Sun card, with cynical instincts and unconvinced of her abilities, expected this behavior of the child/page. Hannah said that although she had accomplished lots of things, the minute she completed a task, she felt as if she hadn't done any of them—even though she had written hundreds of essays and thousands of poems. She felt that part of the problem was an insistence by her parents that she had to be productive. Her artwork, created while sitting and dreaming, was not considered productive by her parents. So she always had to live with the put-downs. "If I could conquer this, I suppose I could go on," she said.

The Three of Pentacles was in the position of her ideals. This card of work and craftsmanship felt neutral. Things were getting done according to plan, but with little emotion. She thought it would be great if she could do this, too. When asked where her project was in the picture, she found it in a little circle in the middle of the three pentacles. This point was at the core or center of everything—the starting point of all the work on the cathedral—but the people on the card were long past this realization and on to something else. She felt she was hiding in the dark shadows. Her book is about the basic starting point of writing—the mystery of where you have to write from—the core material. But would others recognize this? The people in the card seemed fine creating without it. Nevertheless, Hannah felt her essays could help elucidate the core essentials of writing that others fail to recognize.

In the future or next step position, she had the Three of Cups, known for celebration and abundance. She laughingly identified the three figures as her editor and publisher-to-be and her Tarot reader. She also saw them as friends, celebrating and toasting her. She felt her friends (including many of her writing students) were very encouraging: they gave her courage. One of the issues had been that so many of her essays on writing seemed to address a specific group of students and class assignments rather than a universal public unfamiliar with her work. The card suggested that this personal tone, of speaking directly and encouragingly to people she knew, might actually be just what was needed in her book. "That's what the mysteries are about," she said, "a base that gives one heart and courage."

The Magician was in the position of herself as she sees herself. In the Golden Dawn tradition, he is Mercury, the communicator. She said, "Writing is a magical art. You can transform anything with a few words. Also, he grows a lot of flowers—there's a vitality, it's life-giving, and not just magic." Her essays could be the lilies, and her poems the roses. But they must be done by herself—alone, cut off from the rest of the world, focused, and not understood. She didn't know if she could make herself understood. When her book of poems had been published it should have been a celebration but she found it very hard.

The Seven of Swords reversed was in the environment section of the spread. Upright, he seemed frivolous, jolly, lacking focus, and not capable of doing much of anything. Hannah saw him as surrounded by tents full of people—in the world, a part of life. She knew that the card usually meant stealing, but she saw it instead as a sword dance. When reversed, the figure became weaker, a dreamer, moving in his sleep. If the Magician was in this environment he would feel vacant, and just as she felt: overwhelmed by everything going on so that all she wanted to do was steal away (even though she enjoyed the partying aspect of the Three of Cups).

In the position of hopes and fears was the Empress reversed, a classic card for mother issues, but also vacillation and infertility. Hannah saw this card when upright as pretty, hopeful, with the same flowers as in the Magician's garden and with stars on her head. She seemed calm, relaxed and sure of herself. When reversed, it appeared as if her guts were churning, like she was missing an arm—she became grotesque. If Hannah acted like this reversal she would be left alone and could maybe get some work done. It was like a twisted mess was all around her when it should be straightforward. The reversal turned the Empress neurotic, icky, shitty. Still, by getting into it, she should be able to face it and get through it by saying, "Okay, this is hard for me, it is really hard to accept that it's going to be a battle." The danger was in getting thrown back into the Page of Pentacles, where it just wasn't worth it.

The last card, the Queen of Pentacles reversed, was like a combination of the Empress and the Page of Pentacles. It asked, "How can you do this project royally?" However, the reversal indicated a continued uncertainty and mistrust of her ability to produce the book. When upright, Hannah felt the queen was really lovely, humble, and beautiful. She couldn't understand how she had overlooked her when picking a significator. The pentacle on her lap was "more real" than that of the page, and the queen was attending to it as if it were a baby. When reversed, if her qualities were not appreciated, she would descend into deep despair. It was the part of Hannah that really wanted to nurture the book but was not encouraged by her parents, especially her mother who wanted immediate products. It was easy for her to keep the focus for a short time like the Magician—to write a poem, for instance—but she couldn't sustain it for a longer time. It was hard for her to keep supporting, nurturing and cherishing herself on a day-to-day basis. She was good for the short haul like the Magician who did things quickly. "My mother was the one for whom I had to be productive and more extroverted. She wanted me to be happy. I always had to have lots of friends, but I wanted just one friend. I didn't really want all that other stuff. It was a lack of understanding of what I was." If Hannah could tell her mother to stop, she would say, "Stop trying to make me into someone I'm not. Stop trying to make me play with Lucy, I don't like her. And don't make fun of my dreams." It seemed Hannah was still saying these things to her mother—but now it emerged as resistance to her project.

When asked with what cards the Queen of Cups, her significator, felt most comfortable, Hannah responded, "I thought she would be friends with the Queen of Pentacles, but then she fell in love with the Page of Pentacles—they were attracted to each other in some weird magnetic way. He would understand something about her and be very comforting and affectionate. It's almost like he could step through that water, even across the ocean, to her." The pentacles cards were able to value the qualities of the Queen of Cups.

The major arcana cards in the spread—the Magician, Empress, Hermit, and Sun—were different creative modes that she had to express: her poetry, book project, going within, and satisfying her ego out in the world. None of them could be cut off so that only one (the Empress) could achieve. The Empress reversed represented her trouble nurturing a book through a symbolic nine months of gestation to birth. She feared that each of the other major arcana drew away from the energy she needed to write a book, but they shouldn't be sacrificed. The question was how could these major arcana support the Empress without losing themselves or endangering their own inherent value when the Empress's negative energy took over.

If she could remove any one card from the spread, Hannah would remove the Seven of Swords since it represented an energy drain and a stealing of her time. Normally she would handle this with the Hermit, retreating to the quiet of her home to light a candle. The Empress would be more direct, forcing her to face the book and be productive, but there would be danger of her falling into negativity. The Magician could support her by quickly doing one thing at a time, and by reminding her that she can always produce a poem.

By this point Hannah was amazed that she had chosen the Queen of Cups as her significator. "She scares me now, as someone in the past who is too much on the edge. I would regret losing her, but she's a piece of the past." The Queen of Pentacles was more glowing, alive, and beautiful. By comparison the Queen of Cups was cold and blue, and Hannah felt the weird demonic chalice would only speak to her in a robotic way.

The qualities Hannah most wanted to develop in herself were expressed by the upright Queen of Pentacles who could take on the book project without battling about it. Rooted on high ground, she could hold the project in a loving, calm, and grounded way with less fear of being overwhelmed by emotion, allowing her to be more "thoughtful." Because of its reversal, she would have to work with it consciously and deliberately.

Although the advice was minimal and she already knew most of the inner dynamics, Hannah felt that the reading clarified the most important issues and indicated where she should focus her energies. Most significantly, she had laughed and cried as she experienced all the things she talked about, resulting in a transformation of her own self-image (from Queen of Cups to Queen of Pentacles) and an expansion of her possibilities.

CHAPTER EIGHT

Build Your Own Court

This chapter is for everyone who's ever thought of making their own Tarot deck. (Come on, admit it, you have, haven't you?) Even if you are not thinking of designing decks for publication, at one time or another the creative urge will likely assert itself. Most Tarot devotees eventually find themselves with deck design ideas floating around in their heads, and may even commit those ideas to paper. Making your own deck is a wonderful exercise, forging an intimate understanding of the nature of the cards. Many people make a deck for their own personal use. Who knows, you may even find there is a market for your work. Even if you have not thought of making your own deck, this chapter can offer insights into the thought processes behind the design of the court cards in the deck you use.

The court cards are sometimes a struggle for the deck designer and usually he or she will focus on major arcana instead. The major arcana seems to have the most powerful pull on the imagination, and many new decks are inspired by a reconceptualization of the majors. In reality, the courts provide ample opportunity for fresh creativity—look at how many different court card systems abound in modern decks. This chapter gives some new ideas on where to start when designing your own deck.

Often an inspiration for the court cards comes early in the design process. Perhaps there is a card with which you have always connected. You may have a clear image of what it ought to look like. Or perhaps you've come across an image from elsewhere (a famous person, fictional character, etc.) that just seems perfect for one of the cards. These are wonderful sources of ideas, and it is important to record them in your journal or deck design notebook. For instance, if you were to create a *Harry Potter* or *Lord of the Rings* Tarot deck, who would the court cards be?

One of the things that makes the Tarot such a rich divination system is that it has an internal structure—in fact, it has many internal structures. No card exists in isolation, but rather as part of a web of relationships with other cards. The Knight of Cups, for example, shares something with the other knights, and also shares something with the other cups. These connections are of great value in reading the cards, and a good deck design exploits them by using recurring symbolism and systematic parallelism and contrast between cards. Parallelism is evident when all the knights ride horses or the kings and queens wear crowns. Contrast is evident when the four horses are in different stances that are characteristic of their suit qualities.

This chapter will help you use some of the structure underlying the Tarot court cards and combine that structure with your own personal ideas about the cards to create a court that is not only interesting card by card, but also rich in associations and relationships.

This chapter assumes that the basic structure of the courts will follow that of the traditional Tarot, four ranks and four suits. This is not meant to discourage innovation. Some of this material can be adapted to different basic structures, or you may find inspiration for your own system elsewhere.

Quaternities and Suits

The basic structure of the Tarot court is a 4 x 4 matrix, that is, four suits multiplied by four ranks. Geometrically, four is the number of a square or diamond: four corners, four directions, four walls. It is a number of order and stability. Think of the Emperor, in fourth card in the major arcana. Many of our words relating to law, order, and morality have their roots in the stability of the four-fold structure. Our word "right," for example, derives from the Latin *rectus*, meaning "straight," and referring to the right angles and straight lines needed to lay the foundations of temples and other public buildings. Ensuring that these operations were done correctly (another derivative of rectus) was the job of the king (*rex* in Latin). Just a few other derivatives of this root merit attention: erect, direct, regiment, rectify, ruler (both meanings), rectangle, regulate.

The right angles of a square are built on the intersection of perpendicular lines. Nearly every human culture conceives of geographical direction in terms of the cardinal points: north, south, west, and east arising out of two crossing axes. The elemental correspondences of the four Tarot suits are based on such a model, with fire and water as opposite poles of one axis, and earth and air as opposite poles of the crossing axis. The ancients went further, identifying qualities that were shared by neighboring elements, like so:

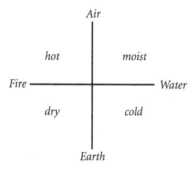

Thus earth is cold and dry, fire is hot and dry, etc. This structure can be an inspiration in developing quaternities of different types. Note that fire and water do not share any qualities and therefore can be seen as opposites; the same with air and earth. If you can think of two sets of opposing qualities, you can either map those four qualities directly to four suits or ranks, or combine them to form the characteristics of those suits or ranks (such as "cold moist" or "mature masculine").

Some care needs to be given to how we apply the concept of opposites in creating a Tarot deck. It is easy to fall into positive / negative contrasts, like love versus hatred, truth versus falsehood, or happiness versus sadness. Although it might be interesting to design a Tarot deck with suits or court card ranks that have strongly positive or negative associations, this is not usually the preferred approach. In most Tarot decks, each card represents aspects of life that can be either beneficial or detrimental, depending on context. This allows for richer readings and offers more emotional and philosophical subtlety. One useful way to think of opposite qualities is in terms of *contraries*, as the term was used by the poet William Blake. Contraries are related qualities in creative tension. As we are drawn toward one, we become conscious of the need for the other. They are like yin and yang, needing each other and complementing each other.

Suppose, for example, one is focusing on the ideas of truth and love as fundamental dimensions. Each of these could be seen as an axis with two poles. We might think of falsehood and hatred as opposites of truth and love, or perhaps instead think of ignorance and loneliness as the absence of truth and love. These four might make interesting suits for a Tarot deck, just as they stand: truth, love, ignorance, and loneliness. Or we could go on and look at the four pairs: truth and love, love and ignorance, ignorance and loneliness, loneliness and truth. Can you think of a single word for each of these four combinations?

Suppose, for example, one is looking at two dimensions of life: the interpersonal and the cognitive. On the interpersonal axis, we might find complementary qualities in the notions of relationship and solitude. These words are both basically neutral, although, of course, an individual might appreciate one more than the other. For most of us, they probably pass the test of contraries: does too much of one make us need the other? On the cognitive axis, instead of using overloaded terms like "truth," we can be more focused, perhaps using reasoning and intuition as complementary ways of thinking.

These four qualities—relationship, solitude, reasoning, and intuition—would themselves make very interesting core concepts behind four suits or four ranks. But to illustrate the process of combining qualities into elements, let's take the example a step further. Imagine the four combinations of qualities: relationship + reasoning, reasoning + solitude, solitude + intuition, and intuition + relationship. There is no single correct answer to what these combinations represent, but here is an example of how one might think about them.

- Relationship + reasoning. This suggests clarity of thought in interacting with others. A good keyword for this element might be communication.

- Reasoning + solitude. This could be about introspection, self-analysis, forming an accurate model of oneself. The keyword might be identity.

- Solitude + intuition. This combination makes one think of meditation, imagination, and spiritual insight. Vision might be a keyword.

- Intuition + relationship. The holistic, intuitive approach to relationships may exhibit sentimentality, idealism, and emotion. A keyword that suggests itself is romance, in the broad sense of the word.

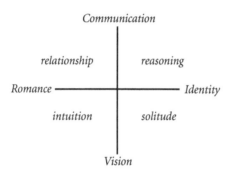

Finally, one could think of concrete symbols to represent each of these elements. We could use scrolls for communication, candles for identity, crystals (perhaps crystal balls!) for vision, and rings for romance.

Quaternity Exercise

In this exercise, you'll create a set of Tarot suits out of a quaternity of complementary qualities, just as we did in the preceding discussion. Even if you are using traditional suit systems, like wands/cups/swords/pentacles, or have already devised an original suit system, this exercise can still be fun and productive. You might ask yourself how the four qualities you develop here correspond with the suits you are already using.

List some qualities that carry meaning for you. Be inventive. You may want to take a day or two to let ideas stew. As you go about your day, notice what things have a strong impact on you (pleasant or unpleasant), and ask what quality of the event you are responding to.

Now, for each quality, write down its complement, or contrary. Now pick two of these pairs to build a quaternity. Using the suit design worksheet at the end of this chapter (page 169), enter the pairs of opposites on the lines in the gray boxes (like hot/cold and dry/moist in the elemental diagram above), and then think of a keyword for each combination of qualities, and note it in the appropriate line on the diagram (left, right, top, or bottom). You've just created a quaternity of suits out of two qualities and their opposites, complements, or contraries.

Now think of how each of those new suits will work in a Tarot deck. If your keywords are abstract (as they are likely to be), think of a concrete object that could symbolize the element. These can be your suit symbols.

You might want to repeat the exercise using qualities you didn't choose the first time.

Keep your mind open to the presence of quaternities in your world. It is surprising how often groupings of four come up in different contexts. There are the four houses at Hogwart's school in the Harry Potter books by J. K. Rowling, four shamanic archetypes in *The Fourfold Way* by Angeles Arrien, four members of the Beatles, four canonical gospels, four fundamental forces in physics, and four "basic food groups," to name just a few.

Ranks and Cycles

Quaternities generated from pairs of qualities in this way have an interesting property: they are also cycles. We can move from one element to the adjacent one just by changing one of the qualities. So for example, fire becomes air by replacing dry with moist, and air becomes water by replacing hot with cold. We can go all the way around the diagram, changing one quality at a time, until we come back to our starting point.

A cycle is thus another pattern that can be conceived of in four parts. An obvious example is the four seasons of spring, summer, autumn, and winter. Then there are the stages in the growth of a plant: seed, leafing, flowering, fruiting. When we arrange a quaternity in a square or cross, it is naturally to apply it to the suits of the Tarot, as we did in the exercise. When we think of a quaternity as a cycle, though, we are coming nearer to the idea of a progression, which relates more easily to the ranks of the court. (There is no reason that the elemental cross idea cannot be applied to ranks, of course. The Golden

Dawn system does precisely that, by assigning the classical elements of earth, water, air, and fire to ranks as well as suits.)

Many cycles can be related to the cycle of life: birth, growth, fruition, and death or decay. "Decay" is a word that has many negative connotations, but we should remind ourselves that it is really the process by which what is created in one cycle returns to feed the next. So it is a kind of giving back. This part of the cycle may not be as obvious to us as the others, and we may see only an ending, not a return and closure. Even power hierarchies can be cyclic as this classic story about a stonecutter demonstrates.

The stonecutter worked all day carving blocks of stone from the mountainside, envying the rich man he worked for. He wished to be the rich man, and his wish was granted. But as the rich man, he resented the sun, which would beat down on him, causing him to suffer from the heat as he made his daily rounds to direct those who worked for him. So he became the sun, only to be affronted by rain clouds that would appear and prevent him from shining on the earth. So he then became a rain cloud, which in turn was blocked and dispersed into rain by the mountain. So at last he became the mountain, only to find himself being chipped away at by the stonecutter!

With a little creativity, it is even possible to see cycles in hierarchies and hierarchies in cycles. Perhaps the king in the traditional Tarot court is more dependent on his servants (the pages or foot soldiers) than he appears to be at first glance!

Progression Exercise

Identify a sphere of activity that is important to you, or that is important to the concept of your deck. It might be spiritual growth, for example, or interpersonal relationships, or work. Now see if you can identify the life cycle of birth, growth, fruition, and decay (or giving back) in that sphere of activity. Give appropriately descriptive names to those stages. Finally, find a word to describe a person who is engaged in each of those four stages (like baby, student, parent, elder). How do these four sound as court card ranks? If they seem a little mundane, you might see if you can find more poetic labels that say much the same thing, perhaps drawing on a different time or culture to give more atmosphere. Do you see a cyclic connection between the first and last rank, or does it seem more like a break?

You might want to repeat this exercise for several different spheres of activity, and select the most appealing ranks from each. Think of different kinds of cycles and developmental progressions. What rank titles might apply to them?

If you like the suits and ranks you found through these two exercises, you may want to record them on the worksheets provided at the end of this chapter (page 169) or in your notebook or journal. Now try integrating both suit and rank together. Obviously, the more sets you've come up with the more likely you are to find interesting combinations.

Real People

We've been dealing so far with abstract concepts: qualities, elements, cycles, progressions. However, if the court cards are going to fill the same niche they do in most Tarot decks (representing people or aspects of our own personality), then they need human characteristics, and these characteristics should reinforce (for you, and for others too if you are thinking of sharing your work) the abstract meanings that may underlie your system.

Real people have an almost infinite range of characteristics that distinguish us from one another. Sex, age, ethnic or racial type, and cultural background are just a few that we learn to be aware of at an early age. In Tarot decks, these physical characteristics are often used as symbols of the more abstract qualities of personality, role, and relationship. (Some decks show red-haired people in the suit associated with fire, just to give one simple example.) This is not always a comfortable territory for the deck designer, as it can feel like stereotyping. Some designers eschew the use of physical characteristics to convey meaning, choosing images that convey the personality they see in a given card, without thought to age, sex, or other attributes. For instance, it would be interesting to design court cards based on the Myers-Briggs Type Indicator (see chapter 4), but how would you convey them without specific sex or age characteristics?

The Tarot, however, is a visual and symbolic medium, and it is helpful if the visual images in the cards draw from a consistent symbolic lexicon. Most Tarot readers are comfortable with the notion, for example, that a child can symbolize innocence, without believing innocence to be the exclusive prerogative of children in real life. Gender and race issues are somewhat more problematic, but the concerns and approaches are similar.

An interesting alternative is to use animals on the court cards. Animals can strongly convey qualities of personality, but using animals gets away from issues of stereotyping. (Actually, it doesn't, but animals are less likely to complain about being stereotyped than humans are.) The idea might be extended to plants or even nonliving things, but this would make it very difficult for many readers to see them as people or personalities. A few deck creators have eschewed the whole issue by using nonhuman symbols to show developmental stages, leaving to the major arcana the entire burden of identifying individuals.

It may be helpful to think of the Tarot cards as windows onto archetypes. An archetype is an innate pattern or basic form deep in the psyche, through which we experience the world. An image is not an archetype, but it may suggest the underlying archetype to us. Which images give us access to a given archetype depends somewhat on our cultural background and personal experience, although there are definitely some archetypal images that span many cultures. Although there might be a person or two for whom an angry young man on a charging horse would suggest the nurturing, care-giving energy of the mother archetype, for most of us, such an image would be a barrier to a mother archetype interpretation. So although the designer may have the perfectly laudable objective of showing that angry young men on horses can also be loving parents, users of such a deck would probably get that message only through studying the designer's written explanations, not through direct response to the imagery, which is the primary channel through which most readers connect with their cards. Use images that speak to you on a nonverbal level and don't require explanation; it is likely they will speak to others too.

Attributes

With these caveats aside, it is now time to consider how we might group people into categories for the purposes of designing court cards.

Sex is an obvious distinction that can be put to use in constructing a court. The distinction between king and queen goes back to the earliest Tarot decks. The *Cary-Yale Visconti* deck from the early fifteenth century extends the gender symmetry to the other ranks as well, including both male and female knights and male and female pages in each suit, for a total of twenty-four court cards! Although there don't appear to be any decks that have all-male courts in some suits and all-female courts in others, the Minchiate does have female pages in the suits of cups and coins, and male pages in the suits of staves and swords.

Because there are two sexes, not four, the use of sex as a marker of rank raises some interesting possibilities. In older decks, the queen is generally the only female court card. The Golden Dawn and Thoth decks, and decks modeled on them, rectify the gender imbalance by using a female princess rather than a male page. This produces a quaternity built on the qualities male/female and parent/child. It might be thought of as two parallel progressions: princess–queen and prince–knight.

If you use sex as a distinction in your court system, give some thought to the interplay between sex and rank, and what implications a given choice might have.

Age is a second obvious distinction that can be put to use. Two age groups can be combined with two sexes to give a symmetrical system of ranks, or you can use four distinct ages.

Age and sex are a powerful combination of attributes. They are human universals, apply to everyone, and strongly evoke our most important relationships: parents, children, lovers, friends, etc. Even if you decide not to use these two qualities to distinguish your court card ranks, you should give conscious thought to how they will make an appearance. They are bound to be noticed, even if you deem them secondary.

The court cards can also be distinguished by more culturally specific attributes. In old Tarot decks (and indeed in playing cards), a few simple symbolic details determine rank: the king is crowned (and usually seated), the knight is mounted, and the jack or foot soldier is standing and has no crown. Such details can be helpful in nontraditional decks too. You might have settled on ranks named child, explorer, healer, and sage. Is there some way to consistently mark these ranks symbolically, across all four suits? You might show one rank consistently in profile, for example, or use differences in clothing, or an animal companion. For instance, Waite and Smith designed their knights so that "the motion of the horse is a key to the character of its rider."[1]

Attributes Exercise

If you have keywords or concepts already identified for the suits and ranks of the court cards, the following exercise may help you translate those ideas into concrete images.

Go through the suits in your mind, one by one. Without thinking too hard, quickly jot down on the suit design worksheet (page 169) any associations that come to mind between the suit and concrete imagery. Cups may make you think of mist, for example. Then, for each suit, think of a color, a posture, a plant or animal, a body type or physical attribute (blue eyes, for example), and an emblem or ornament (other than the suit symbol itself). Feel free to add other categories, too, but stick with concrete things that you can see in a visual image. You don't have to use everything you come up with, so don't censor yourself yet. Just get your impressions down on paper.

Now do exactly the same exercise for each rank in your court system, using the rank design worksheet (page 170). For instance, consider if a different kind of water (mist, stream, pond, ocean) would be helpful in identifying the four ranks within the suit of cups.

Now go back and mark the associations that were especially strong for you —ideas you really liked. Maybe you have strong color associations for each suit, or maybe you see all the queens with cats but have no strong animal associations with the other ranks. Now you can think about how to build these personal associations into the design of the cards (keeping in mind whatever choices you have made about sex and age, too).

Unique Personalities

These exercises have emphasized the 4 x 4 structure of the Tarot court. However, each of the sixteen court cards is also a distinct entity in its own right. The Page of Cups is more than just "cupness" and "pageness" together. You may already have some strong impressions of what specific cards should look like, and those impressions can be incorporated. If some of the cards still seem to lack individual personality, there are many sources of inspiration you can draw from. You can flesh out your court card concepts by assigning specific astrological signs (or other personality indicators) to each card. Think of people in your life (or in books and movies) that capture the essence of the card for you. You might also want to consider unique roles and professions you can assign to the different cards, and work those choices into the illustrations. It is these sorts of details that help the cards come alive and become more than boxes in a table.

Dos and Don'ts

All rules are made to be broken, but it does help to know a few things that will make your court cards easier to identify and work with.

While everyone has their favorite and least favorite personalities, it is usually a mistake to deliberately make some of the court cards likeable and some very unpleasant. If their unique qualities are clearly defined but remain neutral in value then the person using the deck will react to the figure depicted differently depending upon the situation. This flexibility adds depth and richness to the deck's use.

It's generally a good idea to use a distinguishing element to mark just one suit/rank, or else all four. It works to give only one rank a companion animal, or each rank a different companion animal, for example. But if two or three ranks have companion animals and the others don't, it can be confusing.

You don't want the court cards confused with the major arcana or number cards. Keep the actions, scenes, and background simple and uncluttered. Avoid having more than one person in each card, and that person should be the dominant feature. Subsidiary attributes like plants, animals, emblems, and ornaments should be just that, subsidiary, unless they define major characteristics, as the knight's horse often does.

Court Design Worksheet: The Suits

Quaternity:

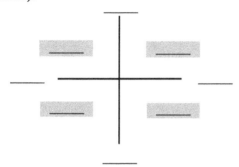

Suit concept and symbol				
Personal associations				
Color				
Posture				
Bodily attribute				
Animal or plant				
Emblem or ornament				
Other:				
Other:				
Final choice—distinguishing attributes				

Court Design Worksheet: The Ranks

Rank concept/name	Sex	Age	Comments

Rank concept and symbol				
Personal associations				
Color				
Posture				
Bodily attribute				
Animal or plant				
Emblem or ornament				
Other:				
Other:				
Final choice— distinguishing attributes				

ENDNOTES

1   *Pictorial Key to the Tarot* by A. E. Waite, p. 174.

CHAPTER NINE

Court Card Interpretations

These meanings were compiled from a wide range of traditional and modern sources, so they are sometimes repetitive, other times divergent or even contradictory. Some terms apply to all cards of the same rank or suit. Still, consistent themes emerge for individual cards, and the variety of interpretations reminds us of the nuances of meaning to be found in each card. Traditional meanings are largely from the eighteenth and nineteenth centuries and may occasionally sound archaic. Styles and occupations are sometimes drawn from corresponding Meyers-Briggs typology.

These lists should be read as a flow of ideas out of which, in any reading, you might emerge with a general sense of characteristics, or you might be drawn to specific themes or words. Only a couple of the many meanings will be applicable in any situation. For instance, the advice section will serve best in advice positions like "What should I do next?" Generally, it suggests acting (or, if reversed, not acting) like that court card would act—the text should only be examples.

These meanings are meant to stimulate your own ideas. If you've done even some of the exercises in this book, then you'll have lots of personal material to add to what you find here. Write in the names of people and aspects of yourself that you associate with each card. Agatha Christi's Miss Marple, the elderly detective, solved most of her crimes because she recognized in strangers personality types similar to those she knew so well from her own village. In readings for others you might find it helpful to consider if they are acting like "so-and-so" would when confronted by a similar situation.

Clockwise from the top left, cards from The Robin Wood Tarot, The
Pythagorean Tarot, The Ancient Tarots de Marseilles, *and*
The World Spirit Tarot.

Page of Wands

TYPICAL ROLES, MASKS, SUBPERSONALITIES

Child; inner child; *puer/puella*; student or new learner; envoy; agent; bringer of news; catalyst of change; subordinate; devotee; bard/entertainer; stranger; new acquaintance.

PERSONALITY STYLES AND VALUES

Ardent; fervent; zealous; energetic; enthusiastic; playful; outgoing; daring; impetuous; brilliant; courageous; curious; intrigued by the new; naïve; trusting; candid; ambitious; takes risks; enterprising; admires and idealizes others; frank; grabbing the tiger by the tail (grasping new opportunities).

STRESSES, PROBLEMS, WEAKNESSES

Bad or incomplete news; selfish; spoiled; delinquent; gullible; moody; unreliable; overly hasty; impatient; hyperactive; easily frustrated or angered; pretended indifference; dilettante; faddish; show-off.

SAMPLE OCCUPATIONS

Student; subordinate; apprentice; telemarketing; creative endeavors; experimentation; investigation; work with new ideas; journalist; information and news specialist; announcer; employment with an influential person; mail worker; sports.

EVENTS, SITUATIONS, ACTIVITIES

The unexpected; thoughts and feelings about innovative, energy matters; thoughts or feelings about future ideas and possibilities; arrival of messages and news, especially unexpected, marvelous, and good; new possibilities requiring immediate action; a new idea or attitude; educational situations.

ADVICE

Be open to potentials and possibilities; go with whatever is inspiring you; start a new project; give in to your impulses; pay attention to messages; listen to what a child has to say; be willing to take a gamble or go on an adventure; share your passion with others.

TRADITIONAL MEANINGS

Pleasant or good news; wonderful; new cooperations and ideas; marvelous; sincere, but hasty-tempered; extraordinary; unusual; dark young man; unprecedented; surprising; gallant with women; strange tidings; tale; given to flattery; episode; unknown; young man of family in search of young lady; digression; story; consistent; faithful; pleasure; brilliance; little rivalries; courage; likely youthful, and selfish in inclination; enthusiasm; beauty; second-rate; satisfaction; relationship with a well meaning, but over-rash and hasty or sanguine man; easily influenced by others of greater art; good stranger; lover; emissary; prodigy; young friend; an associate; not to be relied on as one would gladly do.

TRADITIONAL REVERSED MEANINGS

Bad news, as of a lost lawsuit; inconsistency; indecision; instability; powerlessness; displeasure; notification; instruction; admonition; advice; anecdotes; chronicle; history; reviews; story, tales, or fables; teachings; precepts; unfaithful; charlatanism; worry; superficial; theatrical; cruel; unstable; domineering; announcement.

Clockwise from the top left, cards from The Robin Wood Tarot, The
Pythagorean Tarot, The Ancient Tarots de Marseilles, *and*
The World Spirit Tarot.

Page of Cups

TYPICAL ROLES, MASKS, SUBPERSONALITIES

Child; inner child; student; *puer/puella*; dreamer; artist; good listener; confidant; friend; young lover; envoy, news bringer; catalyst of change; dependent.

PERSONALITY STYLES AND VALUES

Romantic; dreamy; sympathetic; sensitive; cooperative; charming; aesthetic; gentle; gracious; tender; voluptuous; intuitive; imaginative; psychologically insightful; psychic; wants to serve; loyal; promotes harmony; discrete; meditative and contemplative; affectionate; joyful; adoring; open to love; takes emotional risks.

STRESSES, PROBLEMS, WEAKNESSES

Emotionally vulnerable; overly sensitive and sentimental; naïve; avoids conflict; slavish; dependent on others; gossip; possessive; romantic break-ups; perverse; easily influenced; foppish; indolent; envy; jealousy; seductive; flatters; fawns; boy or girl crazy; sluttish; emotional withdrawal; callous; misuse of love; bubbles in the air; refuses to listen to advice or news; obsessed with New Age claptrap; caught in fantasies; cancellation of invitations; unfortunate in love.

SAMPLE OCCUPATIONS

The arts; service industries; waiter; catering; actor; ministry; counseling; personal development; human resources and personnel; public relations; nonprofits; teacher in arts and humanities; puppetry.

EVENTS, SITUATIONS, ACTIVITIES

Educational situations; messages of love; thoughts or feelings about emotional matters; services rendered; social invitations; dressing up; cosmetic improvements; news of engagement, marriage, pregnancy, or birth; puberty rites.

ADVICE

Be open to love; say yes to an invitation; be romantic, poetic, and/or playful; pay attention to a sensitive, loving child; listen to what your dreams and intuition have to tell you; enjoy an artistic project even if you feel you are unskilled.

TRADITIONAL MEANINGS

Studious; loyal; unselfish; trouble at the beginning of the connection; learning; work; devoted; consideration; meditation; occupation; reflection; sometimes perverse as he blends male and female traits; integrity; probity; application; great esteem; discretion; contemplation; observation; slave of the first attractions of love; willingly offers his or her services; a confidant who may gossip and enjoys pranks; young man tormented by love; loved by women but not always to be trusted; sometimes indolent yet courageous if roused; younger man to whom one feels attached.

REVERSED

A weak youth; easily influenced; inclination; penchant; propensity; attraction; taste; sympathy; style; affection; love; attachment; envy; heartache; jealousy; selfish; charm; seduction; invitation; excessive attraction; consent; flattery; fawning; adulation; deception; a penchant that threatens ruin and leads to final destruction; artifice; luxurious.

Clockwise from the top left, cards from The Robin Wood Tarot, The
Pythagorean Tarot, The Ancient Tarots de Marseilles, *and*
The World Spirit Tarot.

Page of Swords

TYPICAL ROLES, MASKS, SUBPERSONALITIES

Child; inner child (wounded child); observer; *puer/puella*; puzzler; logical, rational self; thinker; truth-speaker; journal writer; victim; envoy, bringer of news; catalyst of change; student; Joan of Arc.

PERSONALITY STYLES AND VALUES

Quick witted; clever; vigilant; dextrous; alert; discriminating; assertive; penetrating; active; audacious; clear-sighted; daring; cunning; inquisitive; insightful; detached; subtle; improvisational; agile; likes mental challenges; firm; examines self and others; aloof; accrues data and information; objective; commonsense thinking; disciplined; practical knowledge.

STRESSES, PROBLEMS, WEAKNESSES

Defensive; on guard; suspicious; paranoid; scathing; secretive; illogical; spiteful; revengeful; cunning; vindictive; ruthless; aimless; caustic; difficulty speaking; dull; likes to hurt or belittle others; hostile; psychological or physical abuse; cutting; creating delays; destructive; malicious or slanderous tales; weak or feeble; misunderstandings; suicidal; unprepared; shamed; moody; fawning; distressing or unsettling news; frivolous; overeager; confrontational.

SAMPLE OCCUPATIONS

Lawyer; soldier; diplomat; spy; action careers: sports, baseball, race car driver, pilot, hunter; police; product designer; intelligence agent; troubleshooter; firefighter; business and finance (that offer flexibility and autonomy); crisis management; technical careers: engineering, chiropractic, medical technician, computer programmer; trades: mechanic, repair, carpenter.

EVENTS, SITUATIONS, ACTIVITIES

Thoughts or feelings about mental matters; news, especially of troubles or danger; secrets revealed; ordeals; rumors spread; conspiracies (real or imagined); trouble with the law or legal situations; thoughts or feelings about intellectual matters; military situations; betrayal by a friend; using a knife, sword, or other sharp instrument; taking exams.

ADVICE

Try out new ideas and technologies; identify and use available tools, resources, and mechanical skills; be wary and defensive when needed and prepared to respond quickly to new situations or problems; stay open to an inquisitive child; challenge your mind with something requiring wit or dexterity; protect your position.

TRADITIONAL MEANINGS

Espionage; betrayal by a friend; curiosity; surveillance; night prowlers and soldiers; investigator; vigilance; difficult preparation; examination; a person to be shunned; speculation; reckoning; a lazy, treacherous youth who exploits others; computation; secrecy; learned; a disciplined soldier but with the nature of an assassin; scholar; stewart; observer; actor; an indiscreet person will pry into the querent's secrets; wisdom; strength; acuteness; subtleness; a man having no love for you and inclined to wrong and hurt you but happily limited in opportunity; dexterity; secret service; vigilance; calculation; note-taking; rivalry in love.

TRADITIONAL REVERSED MEANINGS

A weak, feeble person; an imposter; lack of defenses; illness; a plot; sudden attack; suddenly; unexpected; unawares; unforeseen; astonishing; surprising; extraordinary; pleasant surprise; speaking and acting without preparation; vigilance; support; frivolity and cunning; sickness.

Clockwise from the top left, cards from The Robin Wood Tarot, The
Pythagorean Tarot, The Ancient Tarots de Marseilles, *and*
The World Spirit Tarot.

Page of Pentacles

TYPICAL ROLES, MASKS, SUBPERSONALITIES

Child; inner child; student/scholar; apprentice; collector; employee; *puer/puella*; envoy, news bringer; disciple; catalyst of change.

PERSONALITY STYLES AND VALUES

Watchful; realistic; pragmatic; secure; fascinated; curious about nature; steadfast; hard-working; diligent; focused; deliberate; must see and touch to believe; manages things; examines and considers carefully; cautious; loving; gathers details, data, materials; warm; studious; open to transformation, new opportunities, and new skills; concentration; sensuous; respects the earth.

STRESSES, PROBLEMS, WEAKNESSES

Difficulty learning; lack of interest; dropping the ball; insecure; coveting; bogged down in trivia; hedonism; excessive fault-finding; overwork; neurotic attachments; depression; sentimentality; indolence; exhaustion; littering; disrespect for Mother Earth; defacing; vision impaired; gambling; dissipation; squandering; waste; rebelliousness; bad news.

SAMPLE OCCUPATIONS

Domestics; education (especially elementary); student; bookkeeper; secretary; librarian; curators; archivist; coach; medical technician; childcare; veterinarian; social worker; animal trainer; entertainment; project or special events coordinator; financial speculator; business trader or negotiator.

EVENTS, SITUATIONS, ACTIVITIES

News, especially regarding business, plans, and physical matters; thoughts or feelings about physical, material matters; a job offer; new in a position; on-the-job training; following instructions; pregnancy or birth; new projects; the condition of goods and property; opportunity to make money.

ADVICE

Take risks to achieve a practical purpose or if the situation meets definite goals; pay attentión to a careful, studious child; listen to what your body is trying to tell you; be patient; be conscientious and responsible; follow diagrams or instructions; appreciate what you have; start new projects.

TRADITIONAL MEANINGS

Brunette young man who comes to work for you; study; instruction; work; meditation; application; school; bad company will lead you to gamble; concentration; scholarship; conquest of a rich man who will make her happy; amateur; disciple; unjustified ambitions in money matters; reflection; occupation; economy; management; household economy; rule; will deceive a woman heedlessly; news brought by a child; reflection; a relative who uses the tie for personal advantage; order.

TRADITIONAL REVERSED MEANINGS

Profession; bounty; munificence; luxury; superfluous; liberality; beneficence; crowd; throng; multitude; degradation; debasement; damage; dilapidation; pillage; dissipation; rebelliousness; bearer of bad news; disorder; meddling in other people's affairs; thief; money squandered; prodigality; profusion; waste.

Clockwise from the top left, cards from The Robin Wood Tarot, The
Pythagorean Tarot, The Ancient Tarots de Marseilles, *and*
The World Spirit Tarot.

Knight of Wands

TYPICAL ROLES, MASKS, SUBPERSONALITIES

Adventurer; sportsman; entrepreneur; revolutionary; inventor; questor; entertainer; inspirer; facilitator; vagabond; on a mission; a romantic interest.

PERSONALITY STYLES AND VALUES

Dashing; revolutionary; spontaneous; impetuous; impulsive; dynamic; innovative; dramatic; improvisational; enthusiastic; joyful; open; likes to start things but may leave them unfinished; charming; ardent; exciting; animated; vital; competitive; clever; witty; boundless energy; amusing; entertaining; eager; forward-thinking; future-oriented; motivational; spirited; impromptu; extemporaneous.

STRESSES, PROBLEMS, WEAKNESSES

Not completing projects; love 'em and leave 'em; lacks self-discipline; arrogant; impatient; bored with repetitive tasks, details; unfocused; doesn't follow-through; volatile; self-centered; unpredictable; hasty judgments; willful; headstrong; clowning; flamboyant; reckless; rebels against the stodgy and old; burn-out; destructive; seething.

SAMPLE OCCUPATIONS

Writer; crusader; social services; actor; marketing and planning; stockbroker; business campaigns; entertainment; teaching humanities; counseling; entrepreneurial selling of ideas (rather than things); competitive sports.

EVENTS, SITUATIONS, ACTIVITIES

Departure; the coming or going of energy; travel/journeys; inspirational matters; ruptures; discord; quarrels; changing residence; brainstorming; sports events; theatricals; idealistic "causes"; high energy situations; fast-paced.

ADVICE

Take action; share the enthusiasm you feel for life; speak out on issues about which you feel intensely; take a risk; let sparks fly; explore and present your innovative ideas; make a strong showing of fervent regard for someone or something; do something bold.

TRADITIONAL MEANINGS

Flight; removal; separation; distance; friendly; trip; journey; change of address; abandonment; desertion; emigration; remote; absent; foreign; transplant; evasion; swift; moving into the unknown; transpose; translate; enterprising, fiery man; alteration; disunion; alienation; strong; change of position; hasty; just and scorning meanness.

TRADITIONAL REVERSED MEANINGS

Disunity; quarrel; discord; rupture; misunderstanding; estrangement; row; brawl; rupture; dissension; division; parting; separation; strife; contention; contest; a faction or party; discontinuation; interruption; break in relationships; loan not repaid; unexpected change; money borrowed; cruel; intolerant; ill-natured; for a woman, marriage may be frustrated.

Clockwise from the top left, cards from The Robin Wood Tarot, The
Pythagorean Tarot, The Ancient Tarots de Marseilles, *and*
The World Spirit Tarot.

Knight of Cups

TYPICAL ROLES, MASKS, SUBPERSONALITIES

Lover; helper; consoler; rival; seducer; con man; spiritual seeker; romantic; mediator; inviter; artist; music lover; dreamer; knight-in-shining-armor; lady's man.

PERSONALITY STYLES AND VALUES

Deep feelings; seeks harmony; sensitive; idealistic; focus on dreams and visions; psychic; compassionate; sympathetic; avoids conflict; reflective; nonassertive; creative and imaginative; chivalrous; goals of the heart or imagination; gallant; courtly; worships and adores; congenial; charming; loving; warm; affectionate; in love with love; pleasure-loving; attentive; solicitous.

STRESSES, PROBLEMS, WEAKNESSES

Sugarcoating situations; flighty; impractical; being heedless of facts, or sweeping problems under the rug; easily influenced; addictive or co-dependent; emotional insecurity: using charm, flattery, or seduction to get what you want; moody; duplicitous; selfish; use of sex, drugs, or alcohol to heighten pleasure or to escape from life's harsh demands and realities; jealous; fickle; inconstant; can run a con by playing on people's emotions or by seducing people through their fantasies; cavalier; indolent; out of touch with reality; not disciplined; quixotic; infatuations; guileful; disingenuous; wheedling; unctuous; naïve; unrealistic.

SAMPLE OCCUPATIONS

The arts; higher education; counseling; religious, clergy; communications; organizational and personal development; counseling and therapy; human resources and personnel; catering; TV and movies (creating fantasies); nonprofit executive; trainer; teacher in arts and humanities (especially higher education); con man; public relations and advertising; small business (people- or personal-growth oriented).

EVENTS, SITUATIONS, ACTIVITIES

The coming or going of emotional, psychic matters; visits; invitations; proposals; offers; spiritual, mystical activities and journeys; amusements; relaxations; holidays; out-of-body and dream experiences.

ADVICE

Act from your heart; invite someone out for a romantic evening of pleasure and amorousness; use your imagination and creative, artistic, or musical skills; go after your highest ideals; take your lover candy or flowers; offer a kind and sympathetic ear to one who needs it; express your feelings; be gallant.

TRADITIONAL MEANINGS

Seductive; charming lover; invitation; proposal; advent; arrival; approach; advance; attraction; conquest; landing; meeting; reception; welcome; greeting; access; agreement; drawing or bringing together; compliance; congeniality; accession; adhesion; union; affluence; comparison; similitude; visit; pleasant invitation; amusements; holidays; relaxation; conception of conquest and of victory in love; subtle; crafty; artistic.

TRADITIONAL REVERSED MEANINGS

Guile; seduction; deception; fraud; cunning; duplicity; cheating; knavery; villainy; ruse; artifice; finesse; craftiness; trickery; sensitivity; ingenuity; suppleness; compliance; artfulness; heinousness; atrocity; treachery; slander; crookedness; abuse of confidence; evil and merciless.

Clockwise from the top left, cards from The Robin Wood Tarot, The
Pythagorean Tarot, The Ancient Tarots de Marseilles, *and*
The World Spirit Tarot.

Knight of Swords

TYPICAL ROLES, MASKS, SUBPERSONALITIES

Fanatic; advocate; warrior; champion; top gun; rebel; delinquent; bad boy/girl; rebel without a cause; opponent; problem solver and fixer; overcoming obstacles; strategist; angry young man/woman.

PERSONALITY STYLES AND VALUES

Ability; courage; hot temper; anger; imprudence; cutting through; domineering; forceful; skillful; subtle; promptitude; confrontational and competitive; ingenious; focuses on making a point; dashing; single directed focus; outwardly directed; rapier-wit; long-range planner; analytical; clean-hearted; desire to perfect and improve things; hasty; frank and direct; communicates about ideas; takes charge; charges ahead; takes things literally; thinks, analyzes, discriminates, and measures critically; efficient; clever; sharp.

STRESSES, PROBLEMS, WEAKNESSES

Impatience with and insensitivity toward others; arrogant; attacks; headstrong; extravagant; hasty; overly rational; little need for others; destructive; runs rough-shod over others; impersonal; little tolerance or compassion; sarcastic; critical; ironic; caustic; ruthless; know-it-all; stormy; cloudy thinking; impatient; insensitive; overly defensive; slash and burn; short sighted; conflicts with others.

SAMPLE OCCUPATIONS

Soldier; henchman; bully; assassin; combatant; legal services; executive; administrator; manager; stockbroker; financial planner or investment broker; labor relations; economic analyst; strategist; attorney; business or management consulting; judge; science or math teacher; computer technician; chemical engineering; law enforcement; communications (editorials, critical essays, social commentator).

EVENTS, SITUATIONS, ACTIVITIES

The coming or going of mental concerns; heroic action; rabble-rousing; war; arguments; critical evaluations; setting priorities; quick decisions; time management; rapid and efficient application of ideas or solutions; cutting through impediments.

ADVICE

Follow specific guidelines based on objective standards and reasonable policies; champion those in need; cut through obstacles; lead a crusade; champion a cause; look out for and protect those who are less capable than yourself.

TRADITIONAL MEANINGS

Grudge; enemy; dispute; war; battle; duel; heroic action; fanaticism; attack; defense; opposition; destruction; ruin; impetuous rush; overthrowing; beware of attack or slander; hatred; ill will; officials at the law courts; anger; wrath; subordinate chiefs; skill; courage; hot temperament; bravery; full of ideas, thoughts, and designs; anger; advocates; rebels; promptness; rudeness; ability; courage; firm in friendship and enmity; symbolizes the giver of death, who slays as he creates (can indicate death if close to other cards of fatality); imprudence; fury; valor predicted for a soldier; heroic action.

TRADITIONAL REVERSED MEANINGS

Pickpocket; swindler; cardsharp; to play the fool; imprudence; incapacity; ineptitude; ignorance; impertinence; extravagance; crookery; industriousness; weak; impulsive mistakes; silly; simple; foolish; ingenuousness; nonsensical; ridicule; conceited; vain; extravagant; to live by one's wits; news of a disaster; quarrel; disunion in the family; harsh; malicious; obstinate; unreliable.

Knight of Pentacles

Clockwise from the top left, cards from The Robin Wood Tarot, The
Pythagorean Tarot, The Ancient Tarots de Marseilles, *and*
The World Spirit Tarot.

Knight of Pentacles

TYPICAL ROLES, MASKS, SUBPERSONALITIES

Business person; gardener; craftsperson; designer; observer; sensualist; exercise/health advocate; nature lover; couch potato; handyman; tinkerer; strong, silent type.

PERSONALITY STYLES AND VALUES

Possessive; ambitious; purposeful; practical; useful; responsible; reliable; focuses on the "how to" rather than the "why"; persistent; imperturbable; skilled; steadfast; stable; solid; laborious; hard working; dependable; patient; sensory; generally conservative; common sense; diligent; detail-oriented; pragmatic; physical know-how; deliberate and thorough; health-body awareness; concrete reality; utilitarian; studies facts, data, operations; material-status oriented; reserved.

STRESSES, PROBLEMS, WEAKNESSES:

Unemployed; idle; exploitive; stubborn; intolerant; lazy; overworked; mired; stagnant; resentful; worried; unimaginative; dull; lack of initiative or adaptability; plodding.

SAMPLE OCCUPATIONS

Gamblers; croupiers; fortune hunters; exploiters of women; medicine; social work; secretarial/office work; interior decoration; security; retail sales; craftsperson; mechanic; real estate; farming; service industry: flight attendant, waiter, secretary/receptionist at a hotel or restaurant; driver (heavy machinery, public transportation, etc.).

EVENTS, SITUATIONS, ACTIVITIES

The coming or going of material concerns; propitious occasions; practical travel; investments and finances; tangible work, especially with the hands or mechanics; fieldwork; praxis; bodywork.

ADVICE

Work steadily; use your skills and knowledge; use common sense; be willing to work hard and see a job through to the end; invest what you value most in something that promises a sound return; wait patiently; be realistic and practical.

TRADITIONAL MEANINGS

An active, useful, or brave man; serviceable; beneficial; utility; self-interest; self-concern; lucrative; attractive price; advantageous; gain; profit; important; necessary; obliging; kind; helpful; success due to force, perseverance, and/or will; ambitious; wanting to possess quickly and much; idle; negligent; trustworthy; wisdom; thoughtless conduct; economy; order; acting without reason; regulation; propitious occasions; obliging; strange person.

TRADITIONAL REVERSED MEANINGS

Peace; tranquility; repose; sleepiness; apathy; inertia; stagnation; inactivity; idleness; unemployment; leisure; recreation; play; carelessness; indolence; sloth; placidity; numbness; enervation; discouragement; extermination; an opportunity that you will miss; stagnation; negligent; animal; material; stupid.

Clockwise from the top left, cards from The Robin Wood Tarot, The
Pythagorean Tarot, The Ancient Tarots de Marseilles, *and*
The World Spirit Tarot.

Queen of Wands

TYPICAL ROLES, MASKS, SUBPERSONALITIES

Mature feminine; mother; consort; sovereign; business woman; leader; chairman; patron; protector; expert.

PERSONALITY STYLES AND VALUES

Capable; competent; self-governing; autonomous; independent; faith in self; original; visionary; high standards; impersonal; future-oriented; perfectionist (especially required of self); foresight; resourceful; generous; authoritative; spirited creativity; ardent; mentally and physically fruitful; enthusiastic; dynamic; enterprising; vivacious; dignity; compassionate; warmth; confidence; passionate; powers of attraction; intuitive (as opposed to psychic); clairvoyant; close to nature; personal development; self-promotion; assertive; fiercely protective; dramatic; optimistic; audacious; bold.

STRESSES, PROBLEMS, WEAKNESSES

Opposed to restraint; temperamental; skeptical; controlling; dominating; doesn't like repetitive or detailed tasks; can become scattered; self-centered/self-important; intolerant; jealous; hysterical; quick to anger; proud; obstinate; revengeful; treacherous; unfaithful; pushy; catty; malicious.

SAMPLE OCCUPATIONS

Businesswoman; technical fields: research, engineering, computers, systems; technical sides of medicine; creative: writing, arts, design; higher education and administration; management; professions involving independent research and planning; performance artist; sports; journalist and news reporter; chairing organizations; multilevel marketer; TV-show host.

EVENTS, SITUATIONS, ACTIVITIES

Taking charge; setting new directions; business or organizational meetings; personal development; passion expressed; networking; encounters with fiery women or mothering, nurturing individuals; an inspiration reaching mature fruition.

ADVICE

Take charge; let yourself shine; be audacious; express yourself with boldness; be self-determined and independent; let others know what you want; pursue the ideas about which you feel most passionate.

TRADITIONAL MEANINGS

Countrywoman; companion; feminine charm and grace; lady of the manor; good woman possessing great qualities; virtuous; respectable; sympathetic; understanding when not opposed; loving; agreeable; happy marriage with a dark lady; manners; sweetness; good-natured; chaste; avarice; usury; thrifty; frugal; search for a durable relation; educated; active; great attractive power; artistic; love of money; power of command; girlfriend; steady rule; spontaneous temperament; generous; carefree; sudden changes of mood; pleasure-loving; guards her friend's secrets; economical; gives advice; well disposed to those near her; business success; honorable; marked female influence on the querent, in the way of respect, judgment, or authority; friendly; love of money; genteel woman; meek and mild; witty; kind and generous; civility; gives advice.

TRADITIONAL REVERSED MEANINGS

Good woman; kind; benevolent; obliging; helpful; benefit; favor; courtesy; obligation; possible deceit; infidelity; envy; instability; fickleness; hindrance; revengeful; apt to turn suddenly without cause; domineering; obstacles; misplaced charity; extravagant (sometimes given to the upright); resistance; happy old age; a good and virtuous woman, but obstinate; strict and economical; goodwill but without opportunity to exercise it.

Clockwise from the top left, cards from The Robin Wood Tarot, The
Pythagorean Tarot, The Ancient Tarots de Marseilles, *and*
The World Spirit Tarot.

Queen of Cups

TYPICAL ROLES, MASKS, SUBPERSONALITIES

Mature feminine; mother; consort; psychic; dreamer; artist; poet; romantic; counselor; muse; enabler.

PERSONALITY STYLES AND VALUES

Receptive; emotional sensitivity; inner growth and spirituality; shy; fosters art, beauty, and emotions; psychic; harmonizes; taste and aesthetic sense; depth of experience; warm; gentle; caring; charming; alluring; fascinating; mysterious; otherworldly; nurturing; good listener; medial; reflects; tranquil; expresses feelings and emotions; ethereal; affectionate; kind; warmhearted; musing; delicate; goal is personal satisfaction rather than material outcome; empathic; inspiring.

STRESSES, PROBLEMS, WEAKNESSES

Hypersensitive (to criticism and disharmony); unstructured; unreliable; easily distracted; disorganized; unrealistic; irrational; unambitious; lazy; unfocused; sentimental; gullible; idle; moody; fluctuating; fantasies and daydreams; maudlin; nostalgic; insipid; vague; frivolous; saccharine; self-centered; bemused; wishy-washy; inconstant; oblivious to time and sometimes people; easily influenced.

SAMPLE OCCUPATIONS

Psychic; nurse; healer; therapist; medical assistant (a caregiver); arts; crafts and design; teacher; actor; music; fashion; flower arranger; outdoor work; service; clerical; religious; counselor.

EVENTS, SITUATIONS, ACTIVITIES

Dreaming; going with the flow; making wishes; focusing on what you love; relaxing near the water; creating an aesthetic, harmonious environment; enjoying aesthetic pleasures; encounters with watery women or mothering, nurturing individuals; a feeling within reaches mature fruition.

ADVICE

Follow your intuition; promote a caring, supportive, and affirming environment; let the images flow; cherish your dreams; offer your heart to those you love; daydream or meditate; be sympathetic.

TRADITIONAL MEANINGS

Kind; a fair-haired woman; becoming, seemly, decorous; virtuous; warm-hearted; can be a rival to other women; modest; decent; kind, but unwilling to take much trouble for another; honest; distinguished; devoted; success; much affected by other influences; happiness; a paragon of virtue; pleasure; woman of equivocal character; coquettish; romanticism; sentimental; chaste; woman of beauty and charm; advantage; respectable; loving and faithful woman of voluptuous charms; devoted; honorable; comely; sensuality.

TRADITIONAL REVERSED MEANINGS

A woman of distinguished rank; a virtuous woman; vice; inconsistent and inconstant; dishonesty; depravity; immodesty; dissolute; immoral; corruption; scandal; licentiousness; intemperance; intrigue; dishonor; a married woman of high position offers her love; misconduct; a woman in good position, but intermeddling, and to be distrusted; success but with some attendant trouble; a rich marriage.

Clockwise from the top left, cards from The Robin Wood Tarot, The
Pythagorean Tarot, The Ancient Tarots de Marseilles, *and*
The World Spirit Tarot.

Queen of Swords

TYPICAL ROLES, MASKS, SUBPERSONALITIES

Mature feminine; mother; widow; divorced; single mom; forsaken; intellectual; thinker; writer; researcher; disciplinarian; wicked stepmother; ice queen.

PERSONALITY STYLES AND VALUES

Sad; demanding and aloof, with a penetrating mind; austere; honesty; integrity; frank; severe; reserved; detached; clinical; cool; absorbed in problem-solving; discerning; discriminating; precise; skeptical; ingenious; alert; keen; sharp; self-reliant autonomy and independence; thinks independently; impartial; better at organizing concepts and ideas than people; logical; abundance of ideas; open-minded; values competence; easily detects flaws; develops strategies; directs; anticipates problems, generates solutions; delegates well; process oriented rather than product oriented; keen observer; cuts through masks, defenses, and pretensions; just; mastery of equanimity; rigorous; values honest communication; self-disciplined.

STRESSES, PROBLEMS, WEAKNESSES

Hypercritical; fault-finding; finicky; belittling; demeaning; disparaging; demands accountings; severs when necessary; unyielding; dominating; hairsplitting arguments; dismisses the illogical; sharp-tongued; hurtful; calculating coolness; may be unrealistic about application of theory; detail; subterfuge; too complex and abstract ideas; intolerant of redundancy; clouded thinking; sterility; insensitive to others' emotions; vindictive; insuperable distance; separates; destroys; chastises; punishes; judgmental.

SAMPLE OCCUPATIONS

Architect; computer programmer; research and development; systems analyst; product conceptualizer; physicist; surgeon; pharmacist; scientist; lawyer; economist; psychiatrist; archeologist; academician (especially research); writer; editor; negotiator.

EVENTS, SITUATIONS, ACTIVITIES

Writing; editing and critiquing; disciplining; delegating; making difficult decisions; painful situations; ending, separating, terminating; encounters with airy women or mothering individuals; a thought reaching mature fruition.

ADVICE

Be just and loyal; define what is important enough to be worth the risk of possible loss and pain; analyze before acting and anticipate problems; apply principles of fairness; be honest in personnel matters; maintain your personal freedom and be independent with your opinions.

TRADITIONAL MEANINGS

Widowhood; sadness; sorrow; want; absence; scarcity; barrenness; indigence; poverty; misfortune; empty; vacant; unfilled; unoccupied; idle; dormant; free; loss; the plotter; forsaken woman; malice; Joan of Arc; fascinating, if cruel; subtle; quick; intensely perceptive; sterility; mourning; keen observation; confident; evil wishing; a female enemy.

TRADITIONAL REVERSED MEANINGS

A wicked, ill-natured, and spiteful woman; malignant; malicious; vengeful; cheating; knavery; deceit; trickery; artifice; ruse; crookery; finesse; bigotry; prudery; hypocrisy; intolerance; fanaticism; cruel; deceitful; unreliable; narrow-minded; solitude; does not marry lightly; discord; joy with grief; abundance of worry.

Clockwise from the top left, cards from The Robin Wood Tarot, The
Pythagorean Tarot, The Ancient Tarots de Marseilles, *and*
The World Spirit Tarot.

Queen of Pentacles

TYPICAL ROLES, MASKS, SUBPERSONALITIES

Mature feminine; mother; consort; courtesan; new-rich; a madam; business woman; manager; service provider; maintainer; gardener; animal lover; homemaker.

PERSONALITY STYLES AND VALUES

Generous; economic and material security and well-being; liberal; factual; hospitality; femininity; sensuality; practical; capable; preserves; saves; sustains; husbands; cultivates; guards; protects; enjoys comfort, prosperity, and social prestige; resourceful; well organized; interested in beautifying the body and healthy nutrition; clothing; diets; fruitfulness; fertility; hard-working; sensible; ornate; opulence; procreative; thorough; methodical; concentrates; orderly; reliable; memory for details and facts; organized and systematic; cautious; traditional; environmentally conscious; direct, no-nonsense; tangible products and services; completes projects and tasks; appreciates precision; standards; explicit objectives; nurtures and nurses; tending and caring; pragmatic conservation of resources.

STRESSES, PROBLEMS, WEAKNESSES

Materialistic; gets caught in details and daily operations; narrow; hardened; rigid; embittered; unwilling to adapt; lacks vision or perspective; grasping; overly possessive; demands conformity to "their way"; jealous; discourages innovation and risk; tedious; ruthless use of material resources; covetous; ignores/denies the unpleasant; infertile; stressed by physical frustration and material deprivation; stubborn; controlling; self-indulgent; mean; can be taken for granted; harsh and stern.

SAMPLE OCCUPATIONS

Agriculturalist; forestry; gardener; animal husbandry; the practical arts and crafts; food services; nutritionist; clothing manufacture; systems manager; office work; taxes; accountant; government employee; corrections officer; bank officer; finances; educator; legal and technical work; medicine; warehouse and distribution work; quality retail; interior or landscape design; healer; nursing; caretaker; distributor; realtor.

EVENTS, SITUATIONS, ACTIVITIES

Homemaking; hospitality and caring for others; detail work; appreciation of fine things; sensual enjoyment of surroundings; encounters with earthly or mothering, nurturing individuals; a sensation reaches mature fruition.

ADVICE

Make sure that your own physical needs are met; use your resourcefulness to provide stability, and to safeguard your standard of living; be practical with your time and resources; apply down-to-earth common sense; nurture those around you; be resourceful; safeguard your environment.

TRADITIONAL MEANINGS

Dark woman; rich heiress; severe but generous; courtesan; liberal; greatness of soul; security; safety; economic freedom; opulence; riches; luxury; confident; assured; bold; daring; frank; prosperous; high status; frivolous woman with men at her feet; pretty; loves gossip; sincere scandal; rich and happy; modish things of dress; expensive and rare matters; new-rich; match-making, marriage for a young man; brilliant, gifted woman, fond of social life and friends, perhaps of talent in art or literature.

REVERSED

Bad health; an evil, suspicious woman; doubt; mistrust; disloyalty; treachery; depravity; fickleness; uncertain; discord; revenge; evil; dread; terror; apprehension; illness; timidity; vacillating; hesitant; irresolute; perplexed; in suspense; lack of attention to duty; an adventuress.

Clockwise from the top left, cards from The Robin Wood Tarot, The Pythagorean Tarot, The Ancient Tarots de Marseilles, *and* The World Spirit Tarot.

King of Wands

TYPICAL ROLES, MASKS, SUBPERSONALITIES

Mature masculine; father; consort; sage; guide; hero; tyrant; boss; ruler; businessman; benevolent dictator; leader; advisor; consultant; entrepreneur; visionary.

PERSONALITY STYLES AND VALUES

Witty; generous; autocratic; loyal; stalwart; competent; powerful; virile; enterprising; strong initiative; versatile; agile; resourceful; outspoken; charming; stimulating; infectious enthusiasm; friendly; ardent; honest; fair; optimistic; values creativity and innovation; needs variety; open to challenges and opportunities; anticipates; plans; future-oriented; vision and foresight; dynamic; self-starter; energetic; willing to speculate or gamble; self-made; persuasive; motivates others; self-confident; risk-taking; sense of conviction; handles complex situations; long-term goals; high aspirations; dominates through strength of will; delegates; competitive; sees the big picture; bold; courageous; respected; admired; strong principles.

STRESSES, PROBLEMS, WEAKNESSES

Dislikes routine and predictability; doesn't notice details; acts too quickly; ignores standards and accepted ways of doing things; impulsive; doesn't listen to others; blunt; can be insincere; tactless; reluctant to commit (if it takes away options); undependable; arrogant; inconsiderate; rude; know-it-all; egotistical; intolerant; despotic; dominates by threat of force; controlling; hot-tempered; needs an audience.

SAMPLE OCCUPATIONS

Politician; planning and development; sales director; marketing; advertising; promotion; entrepreneur; photographer; agent; journalist; inventor; corporate executive; TV-show host.

EVENTS, SITUATIONS, ACTIVITIES

Setting goals; leadership and visionary directions; delegating; authority or dominance exerted; direction given; mentoring; advice given; new ideas possibly gone stale or passé; the establishment; the rigidification or passing away of creative interests or enthusiasm; plans made; encounters with a mature, fiery man or boss.

ADVICE

Present yourself boldly and courageously; expect to obeyed; treat your vision with respect by committing to it; rely on your beliefs, foresight, and generosity of spirit; innovate; be generous with others; take responsibility: the buck stops with you.

TRADITIONAL MEANINGS

Country gentleman; a good, correct, and pure man; serious; stern; honest, with good intentions; conscience; integrity; married man and/or father; man of talent; genius; knowledge; education; sincere friend; gives good advice; active; generous; man who succeeds in business; fierce; impetuous; good relations with a mature man; strong mental or moral issues; influence of the male sex.

TRADITIONAL REVERSED MEANINGS

A good, serious man; lenient; indulgent; correct; tolerant; compliant; bad investments; excessive and exaggerated ideas; counsel; advice; deliberation; dogmatism; severe; austere; vicious; cruel; bigoted; brutal.

Clockwise from the top left, cards from The Robin Wood Tarot, The
Pythagorean Tarot, The Ancient Tarots de Marseilles, *and*
The World Spirit Tarot.

King of Cups

TYPICAL ROLES, MASKS, SUBPERSONALITIES

Mature masculine; father; consort; ruler; family friend; minister or priest; guru; professor; occult teacher; sage; wise elder; tyrant; leader; advisor or counselor; consultant.

PERSONALITY STYLES AND VALUES

Motivated to help others through direct action and cooperation; serene; calm; subtle; friendly; sympathetic; caring; considerate; compassionate; affectionate; avoids conflicts and problems; willing to help; can overlook own needs in trying to serve others; protective; co-dependent; enforces rules that are "for an individual's or public's good"; soulful; wise; loyal to family and relationships; placid; guided by instincts and intuitions; established emotions; changes moods at will; imaginative; good-natured; jovial; has hidden depths and currents; can move and stir the feelings of others.

STRESSES, PROBLEMS, WEAKNESSES

Hypersensitive to indifference and criticism; difficulty saying "no"; pessimistic; gloomy; doesn't want to offend or disappoint anyone; deception; sanctimonious; living in a fantasy; nostalgic; passive-resistant; violent; self-delusional; unstable; easily seduced; duplicity; overlooking one's own needs; dishonest; rigid control of or hides emotions; manipulation; telling others what they want to hear; can be overwhelmed by another's pain; using love as a means to power; seasickness; addictions; co-dependency.

SAMPLE OCCUPATIONS

Helping professions; health care; ministry; counseling; artistic; therapeutic and social service; caregiver; education (especially elementary and childcare); fisherman or boat captain; boat captain; business (especially those that provide personal services and interaction); hosting; customer service; sales (especially of tangible goods); hairdresser; service industries.

EVENTS, SITUATIONS, ACTIVITIES

Thoughts or feelings about emotional matters; charities; cultural events; dealing with psychological states; seeing a therapist, counselor, or priest; anything having to do with water or the sea; the establishment of religious practices, artistic traditions, or emotional bonds; the rigidification or passing away of the heart and soul; encounter with a mature, watery man or a father or boss.

ADVICE

Nurture, guide, and support others; act socially responsible; let yourself be touched and moved; soulfully express your sentiments and feelings; listen to others with sympathy and understanding; use intuition in decision-making.

TRADITIONAL MEANINGS

A fair-haired, honorable man; fairness; equality; honesty and integrity; religious; fair dealings; kind; responsible; diplomatic in ecclesiastical circles; supportive; affectionate; aristocratic in bearing; generous; lover; obstinate when angered; kindness; liberality; open-handed; business acumen; intuitively wise, but hasty; goodness; chivalrous; take his advice with a grain of salt; considerate; generosity; enthusiastic if roused; poetic; indolent; hypocrisy pretending to help; judgments involving ill will; an intimate friend.

TRADITIONAL REVERSED MEANINGS

A man of business or in office; a dishonorable man; double-dealing; extortion; embezzlement; bribery; injustice; highwayman; robber; thief; rogue; cheat; swindler; vice; corruption; injustice; scandal; ruin; shifty in his dealings; distrust; doubt; suspicion; sensual; idleness; untruthful.

Clockwise from the top left, cards from The Robin Wood Tarot, The
Pythagorean Tarot, The Ancient Tarots de Marseilles, *and*
The World Spirit Tarot.

King of Swords

TYPICAL ROLES, MASKS, SUBPERSONALITIES

Mature masculine; father; consort; boss; ruler; police; judge; government officials; military; tyrant; guide; hero; leader; advisor; executive; diplomat; philosopher; dictator.

PERSONALITY STYLES AND VALUES

Commanding; power; authoritative; controlling; judging; tactical; expeditious; diplomatic; quality control; precision; measuring; cautious; discriminating; discerning; highly rational; abstract thought; enlightenment; scientific methodology; intellectual agility; cool; clear; decisive; dispassionate; impartiality; honesty; severe; disciplinarian; ordered; efficient; upholds standards, morals, and ethics; responsible; committed; logical; full of ideas, thoughts, and designs; analytical; wants clear rules, goals, requirements, and/or deadlines; articulate; eloquent; focused concentration; objective; scrupulously fair; focus on cause and effect.

STRESSES, PROBLEMS, WEAKNESSES

Overly critical; impersonal; unimaginative; rigid; dictatorial; weak; lack of emotion; unreliable or unfaithful; insatiability; unimaginative; arrogant mind; inhumane; feared; cold, uncaring; doesn't listen to others; distrustful; suspicious; cynical; abrupt; argumentative; rude; oblivious to surroundings; oppressive; impatient with others' faults; belligerent; sadistic; cruel.

SAMPLE OCCUPATIONS

Judge; technical writer; corporate manager or executive; lawyer; councilor; diplomat; philosopher; military officer; doctor; politician; debater/speaker; senator; government employee; insurance agent; crime prevention; decision-maker; man of the cloth or lawyer; computer analyst; intelligence services; accountant; security; engineer; physician; auditor; operations and logistics; scientist.

EVENTS, SITUATIONS, ACTIVITIES

Thoughts or feelings about mental matters; trials; battles; prison; dealing with rules and regulations; decision-making; the establishment of laws and limits; strategies and plans; legal situations; the rigidification or passing away of outmoded laws.

ADVICE

Be diplomatic; use your communication skills to defend the truth; clearly define your position; examine the situation for what is illogical or inconsistent, impractical or inefficient; balance discipline with compassion; apply established values or rule; use your experience, knowledge, and discrimination to make wise decisions.

TRADITIONAL MEANINGS

Judge; senator; businessman; jurist; litigant; jurisprudence; power; command; if thwarted he could be an enemy; force; superiority; authority; could lead to dictatorship; unscrupulous; courageous; passionate but unfaithful; active; an enemy; unreliable in business; fierce; resolute; skillful, but inclined to domineer; flatterer; powerful; ambitious; intelligence.

TRADITIONAL REVERSED MEANINGS

Evil intentions; dangerous; an enemy; wickedness; spitefulness; mischievous; ill-natured; perversity; perfidy; crimes; cruelty; inhumanity; atrocities; sadism; chagrin; worry; grief; conflict; disturbance; a lawsuit lost; deceiver; fear; deceitful; tyrannical; crafty; a bad man; barbarity; bad intentions.

Clockwise from the top left, cards from The Robin Wood Tarot, The
Pythagorean Tarot, The Ancient Tarots de Marseilles, *and*
The World Spirit Tarot.

King of Pentacles

TYPICAL ROLES, MASKS, SUBPERSONALITIES

Mature masculine; father; consort; sage; guide; hero; tyrant; boss; ruler; businessman; financier; benevolent dictator; leader; advisor; consultant; patrician; promoter.

PERSONALITY STYLES AND VALUES

Self-sufficiency; success (especially financial); realistic; dependable; business acumen; takes advantage of resources; reason; brawny; resolute; settled; certain; earnest; patient; tenacious; enduring; materialistic; consolidates; conserves; establishes; values possessions and tangible things (especially of quality); loyal; lasting values; conservative; patronizes; concerned with security, quality, and worth; good provider; treasures; looks for excellence and distinction; appraises; valuates; appreciates; pragmatic; jovial; prefers action to conversation, tangible to abstract; likes a good time; humorous; likes good food and wine; strong; attention to detail and facts; potent; powerful; lusty; vigorous; enjoys comfort and luxury; sensual.

STRESSES, PROBLEMS, WEAKNESSES

Usury; unmoving; quick to anger; ruthless; blundering; relentless; bullish; weighty; lethargic; stolid; bunt; insensitive; crude; coarse; crass; uncouth; vulgar; boorish; churlish; philistine; possessive; jealous; lacks vision and foresight; miserly; intolerant; dogmatic; doesn't trust others; patronizing; epicurean; sensualistic; voluptuary.

SAMPLE OCCUPATIONS

Financier, banker; trader, stockbroker (commodities); accountant; mathematician; speculator; investments; car sales; money lender; antiques dealer; merchant; sales; realtor; producer; doctor; civil service: police, firefighter, paramedic, or detective; healer; insurance broker; entertainer; trainer or coach; trade: carpenter, farmer, or general; newscaster; contractor; chef; wholesaler: wine, leather, scent, or fine goods; land developer.

EVENTS, SITUATIONS, ACTIVITIES

Thoughts or feelings about material matters; physical body and health; financial concerns; property; sales and development; establishment of wealth and enduring values; conservation; crafts and skills; the rigidification or passing away of a lineage or way of life; maintenance; encounter with a mature, earthy man or a father or boss.

ADVICE

Pay attention to facts and details; provide a solid foundation for your projects; keep your bargains; spend money and efforts on quality and reliability; consolidate and conserve resources; go for steady, reliable progress; enjoy material and sensory pleasures.

TRADITIONAL MEANINGS

A dark-haired man; able in the areas of the physical body, mathematics, and science; commodities; speculator; loyal; man who may harm you; new-rich; quick to anger but soon appeased; victory; bravery; courage; success; economic power; laborious; ability to forecast; brilliant; honorable; successful; clever and patient in material matters; man of standing with marked taste in art, *belles-lettres*, and the like; gifted.

TRADITIONAL REVERSED MEANINGS

Vice; avarice; lack or deficiency; default; feebleness; weakness; imperfection; corruption; defective shape; deformity; ill-formed nature; disorder; ugliness; irregularity; perversity; stench; an old and vicious man; dangerous; unfaithful; thoughtless and a deceiver; doubt; fear; peril; danger; disenchantment makes him ruthless; a bitter rival or jealous lover.

ℭourt Card Comparison Chart

This chart assumes that the consort of the queen is fire and the companion of the page is air. This is not necessarily the case. Modify the rank designation to fit the court cards in your deck of choice. See the footnote for a more complete explanation of the relationship between the Golden Dawn/Thoth and traditional decks.

	Kings (GD Knight*)	Queens	Knights (GD Prince*)	Pages (GD Princess*)
Element	Fiery part of the element	Watery part of the element	Airy part of the element	Earthy part of the element
Elemental Characteristics	Will	Emotions	Intellect	Physical body/senses
GD Description	Potential power: strong current of activity; swift and violent, soon passes away	Brooding power: steady, unshaken, enduring (protective)	Power in action: illusionary unless set in motion by father and mother	Power of reception and transmission: violent; permanent; material
GD Interpretation	Coming or going of a matter; arrival or departure according to the way they face.	Actual women connected with the subject.	Actual men connected with the subject.	Thoughts or feelings, opinions and ideas, either in harmony with or opposed to the subject.

	Kings Thoth Knight*	Queens	Knights GD Prince*	Pages GD Princess*
Tetra- grammaton	Yod: Instigating Energy	He: Response to and support of the Yod energy	Vau: Working out of the energy.	He (final): Energy materialized
Tattwa & geometric design	Tejas red triangle	Apas silver crescent	Vayu blue circle	Prithivi yellow square
Area of society (de Gébelin)	Government	Religion	History and national characteristics	Arts and sciences
Marital status	Mature married man, or elder	Mature married woman, or elder	Young unmarried man (or indepen- dent woman)	Child; young, un- married woman
Craft standing	Master (of the outer, public). Decision-maker.	Master (of the inner, interper- sonal). Main- tainer.	Journeyman. Explorer.	Student; appren- tice; servant. Obeyer.
Function	Direction; authority	Support; foundation	Travel; departure; change of residence	News, study
Social function	Father; consort	Mother; consort	Adventurer	Messenger; envoy
Service action	Administer; conserver.	Nurturer; caregiver	Action; movement	Catalyst of change
Style	Directive, order- ing, competent, managing, con- trolling, aging, reaching the end.	Magnetic, attract- ing, competent, managing, con- trolling; secure; channels; fosters	Dynamic, aggres- sive, expansive, task- or goal-ori- ented. Chival- rous; cavalier	Take risks; open, naïve, undevel- oped, vulnerable, receptive, in ser- vice; dependent
Develop- mental stage	Fixed, static, or out-moded ideas; Result.	Devotional and developmental ideas. Motivation.	Revolutionary ideas. Overturns outmoded effects.	New ideas; possibilities
Develop- mental function	Finality, comple- tion, letting go, releasing the past, closure	Maturity, compe- tency, fulfillment, authority, skill, understanding	Focus, intensity, involvement, sin- gle-minded di- rectedness	Risk, (re)commit- ment, faith, set- ting out

	Kings Thoth Knight*	Queens	Knights GD Prince*	Pages GD Princess*
Qabalistic world	Atziluth: Creative urge; something seeks to become; direction chosen	Briah: Concept; seed planted; first steps in chosen direction	Yetzirah: Formation; form assumed; shape is known; actions	Assiah: Manifestation; harvest; end or completion of a journey.
Sephirah	Chokmah	Binah	Tiphareth	Malkuth
Aspect of self	Spirit	Soul/Heart	Personal Energies/Mind	Body
Activity	Success; achievement. Dispenses justice and ensures peace.	Sensitivity; introspection. Ensures perpetuity as a channel of incarnation.	Valorous; triumphant. Speed and strength.	Complacent; discreet. A confidant.
Reversed meanings	Overly aggressive or too reticent. Impotent. Arrogant. Doesn't listen to others.	Anxiety; excessive introversion. Reliance on others. Infertile.	Danger ahead. Obstinate. Rebel without a cause. Disloyal.	Difficulties with children. Fearful, closed, reticent. Wounded. Acts out. Tantrums.
Minor arcana number	Fourteen	Thirteen	Twelve	Eleven
Timing	Time for resolute and decisive outer action.	Time for inner reflection.	Time for rapid development and change. Somewhat unstable	Time is not yet ripe, so take your time. Patience, prudence, study/ consideration in preparation.
Card titles	Malik, Re, Roi, Lord, Chief, Patriarch, Master, Father, Guardian, Man, Sage, Resolving, Speaker, Houngan, Exemplar, Shaman, Companion.	Regina, Dame, Reina, Lady, Matriarch, Mistress, Goddess, Mother, Guide, Woman, Sibyl, Lover, Creating, Gift, Mambo, Harvest Lodge, Priestess.	Na'ib, Cavaliere, Cavalier, Caballo, Prince, Mentor, Warrior, Son, Brother, Seeker, Angel, Man, Dancer, Awakening, Knower, La Place, Totem, Amazon.	Thani Na'ib, Fante, Valet, Sota, Servant, Child, Daughter, Princess, Elemental, Maiden, Novice, Seeker, Sister, Seer, Muse, Innocence, Place, Hounsis, Apprentice, Lady, Woman.

ENDNOTES

* The Golden Dawn (GD) and Thoth (Crowley) court cards can never be fully reconciled with traditional Waite-Smith-style Tarot decks, especially when considered elementally. Hence any chart like the one above will be flawed and hard-pressed to serve both systems fully. The Golden Dawn associated the court cards with the Tetragrammaton (the four-lettered, unspoken name of god, *Yod-He-Vau-He*, in Hebrew) which corresponded to the elements and a developmental process so that:

Yod/Fire = Instigating energy

He/Water = Response to and support of that energy

Vau/Air = Working out of that energy

Final *He*/Earth = The energy materialized

This scenario required that the most dynamic, active, and forceful court card come first and be supported by the next card—hence the knight was elevated to the *Yod* or king position as consort to the queen (*He*). To create a balance of male and female, the other two court cards became the son and daughter or prince and princess of the knight (king) and queen. The prince was a king in training (also called the Emperor). Golden Dawn members were told to write these new titles on their continental decks, changing the knights to kings and the kings to princes. Our solution in this book was to consider the queen's consort to always be fire—however, a more precise system that expresses the intention of the Golden Dawn would be as follows:

	Yod/Fire	*He*/Water	*Vau*/Air	final *He*/Earth
GD	King	Queen	Prince/Emperor	Princess/Empress
Thoth	Knight	Queen	Prince	Princess
Trad. (RWS)	Knight	Queen	King	Page

𝕸yers-Briggs Court Card Comparison Chart

This chart illustrates the three ways of creating correspondences between the Tarot court and the Myers-Briggs Type Indicator (MBTI) described in chapter 4 (page 65).

	Mary K. Greer	Jana Riley	Linda Gail Walters
Page of Pentacles	INFJ: The Free Spirit (people-oriented)	INFJ: The Free Spirit	INTP: The Initiator/ Architect
Page of Cups	ENFJ: The Lover (imaginative harmonizer)	INFP: The Dreamer	INFP: The Dreamer
Page of Swords	ISTP: The Professional (practical analyzer)	INTP: The Initiator	ISTP: The Professional
Page of Pentacles	ISFJ: The Builder (realistic adaptor)	ISFJ: The Learner	ISFP: The Listener/ Artist
Knight of Wands	ENFP: The Carefree Spirit (enthusiastic planner of change)	ENFP: The Carefree Spirit	ENTP: The Fulfiller/ Inventor

	Mary K. Greer	Jana Riley	Linda Gail Walters
Knight of Cups	INFP: The Dreamer/Questor (imaginative helper)	ENFJ: The Lover	ENFP: The Carefree Spirit
Knight of Swords	ENTJ: The Thinker or Field Marshal (intuitive organizer)	ENTJ: The Thinker	ESTP: The Communicator/ Administrator
Knight of Pentacles	ESFJ: The Learner/Conservator (sympathetic manager)	ESFP: The Builder	ESFP: The Builder
Queen of Wands	INTJ: The Seer (critical innovator of ideas)	INTJ: The Seer	INTJ: The Seer
Queen of Cups	ISFP: The Listener/ Artist (observant, loyal helper)	ISFP: The Listener	INFJ: The Free Spirit
Queen of Swords	INTP: The Initiator/ Architect (inquisitive analyser)	ISTP: The Professional	ISTJ: The Provider/Trustee
Queen of Pentacles	ISTJ: The Provider/ Trustee (analytical manager)	ISTJ: The Provider	ISFJ: The Builder
King of Wands	ENTP: The Fulfiller/ Inventor (analytical planner of change)	ENTP: The Fulfiller	ENTJ: The Thinker or Field Marshal
King of Cups	ESFJ: The Pleaser/ Seller (practical har- monizer)	ESFJ: The Pleaser	ENFJ: The Lover
King of Swords	ESTJ: The Communicator/ Administrator (fact- minded organizer)	ESTJ: The Communicator	ESTJ: The Communicator
King of Pentacles	ESTP: The Producer/ Promoter (realistic adaptor of material things)	ESTP: The Producer	ESFJ: The Learner/ Conservator

ⓖolden Dawn
Court Card Correspondences

King of Wands (Thoth Knight)

Title: Lord of Flame and Lightning, King of the Spirits of Fire

Elements & tattwas: Fiery part of Fire, Tejas of Tejas (will modifies will)

Zodiac sign & characteristics:
Mutable Fire, Sagittarius

Sephirah & Qabalistic World:
Chokmah in the world of Atziluth

Corresponding card: Chooses
Dominion (Two of Wands)

Decans and dates: Decans 20° Scorpio
to 20° Sagittarius, Nov. 13–Dec. 12

Decan rulers, corresponding cards &
meanings: Venus in Scorpio
(Seven of Cups, Illusory Success)
Mercury in Sagittarius (Eight of
Wands, Swiftness)
Moon in Sagittarius (Nine of
Wands, Oppression)

THE KING OF WANDS

THE KING OF CUPS

King of Cups (Thoth Knight)

Title: Lord of the Waves and Waters, King of the Hosts of the Sea

Elements & tattwas: Fiery part of Water, Tejas of Apas
   (will modifies emotions)

Zodiac sign & characteristics: Mutable Water, Pisces

Sephirah & Qabalistic World: Chokmah in the world of Briah
   Chooses Love (Two of Cups)

Decans and dates: Decans 20° Aquarius to 20° Pisces, Feb. 9–Mar. 10

Decan rulers, corresponding cards & meanings: Moon in Aquarius
   (Seven of Swords, Unstable Effort)
   Saturn in Pisces (Eight of Cups, Abandoned Success)
   Jupiter in Pisces (Nine of Cups, Material Happiness)

THE KING OF SWORDS

King of Swords (Thoth Knight)

Title: Lord of the Wind and the Breezes, King of the Spirits of the Air

Elements & tattwas: Fiery part of Air, Tejas of Vayu
(will modifies intellect)

Zodiac sign & characteristics: Mutable Air, Gemini

Sephirah & Qabalistic World: Chokmah in the world of Yetzirah
Chooses Peace Restored (Two of Swords)

Decans and dates: Decans 20° Taurus to 20° Gemini, May 11–June 10

Decan rulers, corresponding cards & meanings: Saturn in Taurus (Seven
of Pentacles, Success Unfulfilled)
Jupiter in Gemini (Eight of Swords, Shortened Force)
Mars in Gemini (Nine of Swords, Despair and Cruelty)

THE KING OF PENTACLES

King of Pentacles (Thoth Knight)

Title: Lord of the Wide and Fertile land, King of the Spirits of Earth

Elements & tattwas: Fiery part of Earth, Tejas of Prithivi (will modifies physical senses)

Zodiac sign & characteristics: Mutable Earth, Virgo

Sephirah & Qabalistic World: Chokmah in the world of Assiah Chooses Harmonious Change (Two of Pentacles)

Decans and dates: Decans 20° Leo to 20° Virgo, Aug. 12–Sep. 11

Decan rulers, corresponding cards & meanings: Mars in Leo (Seven of Wands, Valor)
Sun in Virgo (Eight of Pentacles, Prudence)
Venus in Virgo (Nine of Pentacles, Material Gain)

THE QUEEN OF WANDS

Queen of Wands

Title: Queen of the Thrones of Flames

Elements & tattwas: Watery part of Fire, Apas of Tejas
(emotions modify will)

Zodiac sign & characteristics: Cardinal Fire, Aries

Sephirah & Qabalistic World: Binah in the world of Atziluth
Gives form to Established Strength—Virtue (Three of Wands)

Decans and dates: Decans 20° Pisces to 20° Aries, Mar. 11–Apr. 10

Decan rulers, corresponding cards & meanings: Mars in Pisces (Ten of
Cups, Perpetual Success)
Mars in Aries (Two of Wands, Dominion)
Sun in Aries (Three of Wands, Established Strength)

THE QUEEN OF CUPS

Queen of Cups

Title: Queen of the Thrones of the Waters

Elements & tattwas: Watery part of Water, Apas of Apas
(emotions modify emotions)

Zodiac sign & characteristics: Cardinal Water, Cancer

Sephirah & Qabalistic World: Binah in the world of Briah
Gives form to Abundance (Three of Cups)

Decans and dates: Decans 20° Gemini to 20° Cancer, June 11–July 11

Decan rulers, corresponding cards & meanings: Sun in Gemini (Ten of
Swords, Ruin)
Venus in Cancer (Two of Cups, Love)
Mercury in Cancer (Three of Cups, Abundance)

THE QUEEN OF SWORDS

Queen of Swords

Title: Queen of the Thrones of the Air

Elements & tattwas: Watery part of Air, Apas of Vayu (emotions modify intellect)

Zodiac sign & characteristics: Cardinal Air, Libra

Sephirah & Qabalistic World: Binah in the world of Yetzirah
Gives form to Sorrow (Three of Swords)

Decans and dates: Decans 20° Virgo to 20° Libra, Sep. 12–Oct. 12

Decan rulers, corresponding cards & meanings: Mercury in Virgo (Ten of Pentacles, Wealth)
Moon in Libra (Two of Swords, Peace Restored)
Saturn in Libra (Three of Swords, Sorrow)

THE QUEEN OF PENTACLES

Queen of Pentacles

Title: Queen of the Thrones of Earth

Elements & tattwas: Watery part of Earth, Apas of Prithivi
(emotions modify physical senses)

Zodiac sign & characteristics: Cardinal Earth, Capricorn

Sephirah & Qabalistic World: Binah in the world of Assiah
Gives form to Material Works (Three of Pentacles)

Decans and dates: Decans 20° Sagittarius to 20° Capricorn, Dec. 13–Jan. 9

Decan rulers, corresponding cards & meanings: Saturn in Sagittarius
(Ten of Wands, Oppression)
Jupiter in Capricorn (Two of Pentacles, Harmonious Change)
Mars in Capricorn (Three of Pentacles, Material Works)

THE PRINCE OF WANDS

Prince of Wands

Title: Prince of the Chariot of the Air

Elements & tattwas: Airy part of Fire, Vayu of Tejas (intellect modifies will)

Zodiac sign & characteristics: Fixed Fire, Leo

Sephirah & Qabalistic World: Tiphareth in the world of Atziluth Quests after Victory (Six of Wands)

Decans and dates: Decans 20° Cancer to 20° Leo, July 12–Aug. 11

Decan rulers, corresponding cards & meanings: Moon in Cancer (Four of Cups, Blended Pleasure)
Saturn in Leo (Five of Wands, Strife)
Jupiter in Leo (Six of Wands, Victory)

THE PRINCE OF CUPS

Prince of Cups

Title: Prince of the Chariot of the Waters

Elements & tattwas: Airy part of Water, Vayu of Apas
(intellect modifies emotion)

Zodiac sign & characteristics: Fixed Water, Scorpio

Sephirah & Qabalistic World: Tiphareth in the world of Briah
Quests after Pleasure (Six of Cups)

Decans and dates: Decans 20° Libra to 20° Scorpio, Oct, 13–Nov. 12

Decan rulers, corresponding cards & meanings: Jupiter in Libra (Four of
Swords, Rest from Strife)
Mars in Scorpio (Five of Cups, Loss in Pleasure)
Sun in Scorpio (Six of Cups, Pleasure)

THE PRINCE OF SWORDS

Prince of Swords

Title: Prince of the Chariot of the Air

Elements & tattwas: Airy part of Air, Vayu of Vayu (intellect modifies intellect)

Zodiac sign & characteristics: Fixed Air, Aquarius

Sephirah & Qabalistic World: Tiphareth in the world of Yetzirah Quests after Earned Success—Science (Six of Swords)

Decans and dates: Decans 20° Capricorn to 20° Aquarius, Jan. 10–Feb. 8

Decan rulers, corresponding cards & meanings: Sun in Capricorn (Four of Pentacles, Earthly Power)
Venus in Aquarius (Five of Swords, Defeat)
Mercury in Aquarius (Six of Swords, Earned Success)

THE PRINCE OF PENTACLES

Prince of Pentacles

Title: Prince of the Chariot of Earth

Elements & tattwas: Airy part of Earth, Vayu of Prithivi (intellect modifies physical senses)

Zodiac sign & characteristics: Fixed Earth, Taurus

Sephirah & Qabalistic World: Tiphareth in the world of Assiah Quests after Material Success (Six of Pentacles)

Decans and dates: Decans 20° Aries to 20° Taurus, Apr. 11–May 10

Decan rulers, corresponding cards & meanings: Venus in Aries (Four of Wands, Perfected Work)
Mercury in Taurus (Five of Pentacles, Material Trouble)
Moon in Taurus (Six of Pentacles, Material Success)

THE PRINCESS OF WANDS

Princess of Wands

Title: Princess of the Shining Flame, Rose of the Palace of Fire

Elements & tattwas: Earthy part of Fire, Prithivi of Tejas (physical senses modify will)

Sephirah & Qabalistic World: Malkuth in the world of Atziluth Gives birth to Oppression (Ten of Wands)

Zodiacal attributes: Rules the second quadrant of the zodiac: Cancer, Leo, and Virgo

Corresponding minor arcana: Is the Throne of the Power of the Ace of Wands

THE PRINCESS OF CUPS

Princess of Cups

Title: Princess of the Waters and the Lotus

Elements & tattwas: Earthy part of Water, Prithivi of Apas (physical senses modify emotions)

Sephirah & Qabalistic World: Malkuth in the world of Briah Gives birth to Perpetual Success (Satiety) (Ten of Cups)

Zodiacal attributes: Rules the third quadrant of the zodiac: Libra, Scorpio, and Sagittarius

Corresponding minor arcana: Is the Throne of the Power of the Ace of Cups

THE PRINCESS OF SWORDS

Princess of Swords

Title: Princess of the Rushing Winds, Lotus of the Palace of Air

Elements & tattwas: Earthy part of Air, Prithivi of Vayu
(physical senses modify intellect)

Sephirah & Qabalistic World: Malkuth in the world of Yetzirah
Gives birth to Ruin (Ten of Swords)

Zodiacal attributes: Rules the fourth quadrant of the zodiac: Capricorn,
Aquarius, and Pisces

Corresponding minor arcana: Is the Throne of the Power of the Ace of
Swords

Princess of Pentacles

Title: Princess of the Echoing Hills, Rose of the Palace of Earth

Elements & tattwas: Earthy part of Earth, Prithivi of Prithivi (physical senses modify physical senses)

Sephirah & Qabalistic World: Malkuth in the world of Assiah Gives birth to Wealth (Ten of Pentacles)

Zodiacal attributes: Rules the first quadrant of the zodiac: Aries, Taurus, and Gemini

Corresponding minor arcana: Is the Throne of the Power of the Ace of Pentacles

ℐmportant Terms

AFFINITIES—A synonym for correspondences used by the Golden Dawn to indicate similar characteristics and forces of attraction between things or ideas.

ANIMA / ANIMUS—Term used by psychologist Carl Jung to indicate the unconscious or concealed female element in the male, and male element in the female, respectively. Their basic function is to inspire.

ARCHETYPE—Archaic remnants of instinctual patterns of meaning in the human psyche that crop up in myth, fairy tales, dreams, fantasies, and art, and influence our psychology. These collective thought patterns are innate and inherited.

COAT CARDS—Another name for court cards.

COLLECTIVE UNCONSCIOUS—Jung's term for the aspects of the unconscious that are universal, impersonal and identical in everyone.

CORRESPONDENCES—Associations between the cards of the tarot and other entities or concepts, such as the four elements, the signs of the Zodiac, or the sephiroth of the Qabalah. There are many different systems of correspondences in use. Some have a longer history than others, but none can claim to be uniquely correct.

COURT CARDS—The minor arcana cards that do not have a numerical value (see number cards), but typically depict people (such as kings, queens, knights, and pages) instead.

DECAN—A ten-degree segment of the zodiac. The Golden Dawn assigned the number cards (aces excluded) to the thirty-six decans, and assigned each court card to three decans overlapping two of the signs of the zodiac.

DIGNITY/DIGNIFIED—Indicates a value or worth applied to a card (or spread), through the appearance of any number of factors that enhance its characteristics (see elemental dignities).

ELEMENT(S)—Before the rise of modern chemistry, Western culture recognized four basic elements, or constituents of the natural world: fire, water, air, and earth. All things were composed of these four elements, in various combinations. The four suits of the minor arcana in the Tarot are often equated with the four elements, although not always in the same way.

ELEMENTAL DIGNITIES—A method of interpreting cards in a spread that uses the correspondences among elements (and thus suits) to identify cards that strengthen or weaken each other.

FACE CARDS—Another name for court cards.

FACEUP/FACEDOWN—*Faceup* means that you are looking at the images on the cards (usually this means that you are consciously selecting a card for some particular reason). *Facedown* is how the cards are usually shuffled and dealt—you are looking at the back of the card and can't see which card it is until it is turned over.

FAN—An optional method for selecting cards for a spread. The cards are laid facedown on a surface and swept to form a curved row with part of each card discernable (like a fan). To select from fanned cards, move your hand above them until you feel drawn to take out a particular card.

GOLDEN DAWN—The Hermetic Order of the Golden Dawn was an occult society active in England from 1888 and continuing in various forms to this day. The group's teachings regarding the Tarot have dominated

Tarot interpretation in the English-speaking world. Two of the group's prominent members, A. E. Waite and Aleister Crowley, designed important Tarot decks and wrote influential books on Tarot.

KING—A court card in traditional decks, usually the highest rank.

KNAVE—An English term for the lowest-ranking court card in a playing-card deck, now often called the jack. The term was sometimes applied to the page in the Tarot deck. A knave is a male servant, but the term is also used in a derogatory sense to refer to someone of low class and disreputable character.

MARSEILLES TAROT (OR TAROT DE MARSEILLE)—A woodcut-style deck that was in use as early as the seventeenth century, becoming the standard divination deck in France and some other parts of Europe. Because of its age and popularity it is sometimes called the "traditional" Tarot, which can be confusing (see traditional).

MAJOR ARCANA—The "special" symbolic cards of the Tarot (usually twenty-two in number), such as the Magician, Temperance, etc., that do not belong to the four suits.

MASK—An outward persona that conceals some or all of one's true personality. We are often not aware of our masks, adopting them without conscious choice.

MINOR ARCANA—The "suit cards" of the Tarot, derived from early playing cards. The minor arcana usually consist of ten number cards and four court cards, in each of four suits.

NEMESIS—A Greek goddess of revenge and justice. Also signifies an unbeatable rival. The term is used in this book to name the court card one identifies with least.

NUMBER CARDS—The forty minor arcana cards that bear a numerical rank, from ace through ten.

PAGE—One of the court card ranks in traditional decks, usually the lowest rank.

PEOPLE CARDS—Another name for court cards.

PIP—A suit symbol appearing on a card (such as a sword or cup in a Tarot deck, or a spade or heart in a playing card deck). The number cards of a Tarot deck are sometimes called pip cards, or just "pips" for short. The term is often used to distinguish the number cards in old decks (which usually show just the suit symbols) from number cards in many modern decks, which are illustrated with pictorial scenes.

PROJECTION—A psychological term for taking personality traits one does not wish to acknowledge in oneself and seeing them in other people instead.

PUER/PUELLA—Latin terms used by Carl Jung to signify the archetype of the "eternal youth," who is unable to commit in a responsible way. Puer is the man who never becomes emotionally mature and puella, the woman.

QABALAH—A Jewish mystical tradition that became very influential in European magical and occult practice. Qabalistic ideas are reflected in the symbolism and interpretation of many modern Tarot decks. (Also spelled Cabala or Kabbalah.)

QUATERNITY—A structured grouping of four things.

QUEEN—One of the court card ranks in traditional decks.

QUERENT—Literally, "questioner," the person who seeks advice or insight from the Tarot cards during a reading. If you read the cards for yourself, you are both reader and querent. If you read the cards for another person, you are the reader and the other is the querent.

RANDOM—Refers to an outcome one does not predict in advance. The presumption that unpredictable events are meaningless, which is the sense often conveyed by the word, is a relatively modern concept. The divinatory arts are based on a different model—that outcomes we do not predict carry important messages. To randomly mix the cards is to rearrange their order in some fashion. To pick a card at random means to draw a card from anywhere in the deck (often by shuffling, cutting, and dealing the cards or selecting them from a fan).

REVERSAL/REVERSED—A card is reversed if it is laid so the image appears upside-down. Reversals are usually interpreted differently than upright cards. Some readers do not use reversals, preferring to keep all the cards in their deck upright, or to turn reversed cards rightside-up when they appear.

RANKS—The individual stations in the court-card hierarchy. In the Waite-Smith deck and many traditional decks, the four ranks are page, knight, queen, and king. In the Crowley-Harris Thoth deck, the ranks are princess, prince, queen, and knight.

READER—The person who interprets the Tarot cards during a reading. If you read the cards for yourself, you are both reader and querent. If you read the cards for another person, you are the reader and the other is the querent.

RIDER-WAITE TAROT/RIDER-WAITE-SMITH TAROT—See Waite-Smith Tarot.

ROLE—A set of behaviors one assumes in order to perform a particular task or meet a particular set of expectations. Examples of roles include bank teller, father, student, friend, gardener. We are generally conscious of the roles we assume. (Compare with mask and subpersonality.)

ROYALTY CARDS—Another name for court cards.

SEPHIRAH (plural: *sephiroth*)—In Qabalah, one of ten states of being on the Tree of Life through which divine consciousness descends into matter, and through which human conscious may rise upward toward the divine.

SHADOW—In Jungian psychology, the aspects of one's personality that are ignored or repressed by the conscious mind. Shadow aspects are often projected onto another person.

SIGNIFICATOR—A card (often a court card) selected to represent the querent in a reading or, occasionally, the subject of the reading.

SPREAD/LAYOUT—An arrangement of cards used for a Tarot reading. The different positions in a spread usually carry different meanings, and each card is interpreted in light of the position where it appears.

STACK—A pile of cards, usually facedown. It often refers to just a section of the whole deck, as in "cut the deck into three stacks."

SUBPERSONALITY—A different set of behaviors or traits that expresses itself under special circumstances, such as stress, in solitude, or with certain people. Masks and roles are examples of subpersonalities.

SUIT—One of the four large divisions of the minor arcana, including the court cards. In the Waite-Smith deck, the suits are wands, cups, swords, and pentacles.

TATTWA/TATTVA—From the Indian tantric tradition, a colored geometric form symbolizing an element or combination of elements.

TETRAGRAMMATON—the four Hebrew letters (*Yod, He, Vau, He*-final) that stand for the name of God and constitute one of the central themes of Qabalah.

THOTH DECK—Tarot deck created by Aleister Crowley and Lady Frieda Harris and completed in 1944. Although primarily following Golden Dawn attributes there are some significant differences, among which the king is called knight.

TRADITIONAL (OR STANDARD)—There is no single Tarot tradition, either in the design of the cards or their interpretation, hence there is always some ambiguity in speaking of a "traditional" deck or "traditional" correspondences. The term is best understood in a relative sense, to distinguish what is relatively older and more established from more recent innovations. Thus, in the context of decks designed in the present decade, the Waite-Smith deck (from 1909) may be referred to as "traditional," whereas in a different context (the design of the pip cards, for instance), the Waite-Smith deck may be contrasted with "traditional" decks such as the Tarot de Marseille (which existed at least as early as the 1600s). There is even less basis for referring to a deck or interpretation as "standard." There has never been a universally agreed-upon standard Tarot, and variety has been prominent in Tarot tradition since the first appearance of the cards.

TREE OF LIFE—In Qabalah, the Tree of Life is an arrangement of the ten sephiroth and the connecting paths among them, a sort of mystical map of creation.

TRUMPS / TRIUMPHS—"Trumps" is a corruption of the Italian *trionfi*, or "triumphs." This is the earliest term for the special allegorical cards of the Tarot deck. (The term was sometimes extended to refer to the deck as a whole, much as Tarot is used today.) A likely source for the word is Petrarch's poem, "The Triumphs," in which a series of allegorical figures are defeated by more powerful ones. "Major arcana" is a modern term for the Tarot trumps, although historically speaking, the "trumps" usually did not include the Fool.

UNCONSCIOUS—Parts of the mind or personality of which we are not directly aware.

UPRIGHT—The opposite of reversed. Unless otherwise noted, interpretations given in this book assume that the card is upright.

VALET—The French term for the lowest-ranking court card, corresponding to the page in the Waite-Smith deck. (It should be noted, though, that a valet is a personal servant, whereas the word "page" suggests a messenger or errand runner. Valet corresponds more closely to the English word "squire.")

WAITE-SMITH TAROT—An influential Tarot deck designed by Golden Dawn members A. E. Waite and Pamela Colman Smith. It was first published in 1909 as *The Rider Tarot Pack* (Rider was the publisher's name). It is often referred to as the "Rider-Waite" Tarot or the "Rider-Waite-Smith" (RWS) Tarot.

WORLDS / QABALISTIC WORLDS—A term for four realms or planes of existence depicted on the Tree of Life: Assiah (material), Yetzirah (formative), Briah (creative), and Atziluth (divine) and related by the Golden Dawn to the Tarot suits and court card ranks.

ℬibliography

Benham, W. Gurney. Playing Cards: *Their History and Secrets*. (London: Ward, Lock & Co., 1931).

Butler, Bill. *Dictionary of the Tarot*. (New York, NY: Schocken Books, 1975).

Case, Paul Foster. *The Tarot: A Key to the Wisdom of the Ages*. (Richmond, VA: Macoy Publishing, 1947).

Cattell, Heather E. P., and James M. Shuerger. *Essentials of 16PF Assessment*. (New York: John Wiley & Sons, 2003).

Cook, Catherine, and Dwariko von Sommaruga. *Songs for the Journey Home: Alchemy Through Imagery: A Tarot Pathway* [deck and book]. (Auckland, New Zealand: Alchemists & Artists, 1993).

Crowley, Aleister. *The Book of Thoth: An Interpretation of the Tarot*. (New York, NY: Samuel Weiser, 1974).

de Castillejo, Irene Claremont. *Knowing Woman: A Feminine Psychology*. (1973; reprint Boston, MA: Shambhala, 1997).

Denning, Trevor. *The Playing-Cards of Spain: A Guide for Historians and Collectors* (London: Cygnus Arts, 1996).

Dummett, Michael. *The Game of Tarot*. (London: Duckworth, 1980).

DuQuette, Lon Milo. *Tarot of Ceremonial Magick* (York Beach, ME: Samuel Weiser, 1995).

Ford, Debbie. *The Dark Side of the Light Chasers* (audio tape: Jodere Group, 2001).

Greer, Mary K. *Tarot for Your Self: A Workbook for Personal Transformation*. (Revised Edition. Franklin Lakes, NJ: New Page Books, 2002).

———. *Tarot Constellations: Patterns of Personal Destiny*. (Franklin Lakes, NJ: New Page Books, 1987).

———. *The Complete Book of Tarot Reversals*. (St. Paul MN: Llewellyn Publications, 2002).

Hall, Manly Palmer. *The Secret Teachings of All Ages*. (Los Angeles, CA: Philosophical Research Society, 1988).

Holy Order of Mans. *Jewels of the Wise*. (San Francisco, CA: Holy Order of Mans, 1974).

Hutton, Ronald. *The Triumph of the Moon: A History of Modern Pagan Witchcraft*. (Oxford: Oxford University Press, 1999).

Keirsey, David, and Marily Bates. *Please Understand Me*. (Del Mar, CA: Prometheus Nemesis, 1978).

Kroeger, Otto, and Janet M. Thuesen. *Type Talk*. (New York: Delacorte Press, 1988).

Lévi, Eliphas. *Transcendental Magic: Its Doctrine and Ritual* (first English translation, 1896, reprint: York Beach, ME: Samuel Weiser, 1970).

Michelsen, Teresa. *Creating Your Own Tarot Spreads* (St. Paul, MN: Llewellyn, 2003).

Moore, Robert, and Douglas Gillette. *King, Warrior, Magician, Lover*. (San Francisco, CA: HarperSanFrancisco, 1990).

Mumford, Jonn. *Magicial Tattwa Cards: A Complete System for Self-Development*. (St. Paul, MN: Llewellyn Publications, 1997).

Myers, Isabel Briggs. *Introduction to Type: A Description of the Theory and Application of the Myers-Briggs Type Indicator*. (Palo Alto, CA: Consulting Psychologists Press, 1987).

Opsopaus, John. *Guide to the Pythagorean Tarot*. (deck illustrations by Rho) (St. Paul, MN: Llewellyn Publications, 2001).

Papus, *Le Tarot Divinatoire: Clef du tirage des Cartes et des Sortes*. St. Jean de Braye: Éditions Dangles, 1993; reprint of the 1910 edition. (Includes the divinatory meanings of Etteilla).

Regardie, Israel. *The Complete Golden Dawn System of Magic*. (Phoenix, AZ: Falcon Press, 1986). [Contains *Book T*]

Riley, Jana. *Tarot Dictionary and Compendium*. (York Beach, ME: Samuel Weiser, 1995).

Waite, Arthur Edward. *A Pictorial Key to the Tarot*. (New York: Red Wheel/Weiser, 1975).

Wang, Robert. *An Introduction to the Golden Dawn Tarot*. (New York, NY: Samuel Weiser, 1978) [Contains *Book T*].

Web Resources

Bonewits, Isaac. Indo-European Caste Systems and Cosmologies.
http://www.neopagan.net/IE_Cosmology.html

du Coeur, Justin. *The Introduction of Playing Cards to Europe.* http://www.jducoeur.org/game-hist/seaan-cardhist.html

Little, Tom. *The Hermitage: A Tarot History Site.* http://www.tarothermit.com

———. *TarotL History Information Sheet.* http://tarothermit.com

MBTI Typology Tests

http://keirsey.com

http://www.humanmetrics.com

Pollett, Andrea. *An Introduction to Playing Cards.* http://www.geocities.com/Paris/Musee/7685/cardsc.htm

The 16PF Questionnaire: Primary Factors—Definitions.. http://www.16pfworld.com/primaryfactors.html

Featured Decks

Ancient Minchiate Etruria. (St. Paul, MN: Llewellyn Publications, 2002).

Cicero, Sandra T. and Chic. *Golden Dawn Magical Tarot.* (St. Paul, MN: Llewellyn Publications, 2000).

Conver, Nicolas. *Ancient Tarots of Marseille.* (St. Paul, MN: Llewellyn Publications, 2002).

Godino, Jessica, and Lauren O'Leary. *World Spirit Tarot.* (St. Paul, MN: Llewellyn Publications, 2001).

Opsopaus, John, and Rho. *The Pythagorean Tarot* (St. Paul, MN: Llewellyn Publications, 2001).

Pollack, Rachel. *The Shining Tribe Tarot.* (St. Paul, MN: Llewellyn Publications, 2001).

Wood, Robin, and Michael Short. *Robin Wood Tarot.* (St. Paul, MN: Llewellyn Publications, 1991).

Tarot Cards 1JJ [Swiss *1JJ*]. (New York: U.S. Games, 1970).

Universal Waite Tarot. (Stanford, CT: U.S. Games, 1990).

$\mathcal{I}$ndex

history. See Tarot history

Holy Grail, 35, 130

household, 27, 29, 31–32, 34–37, 48, 140, 185

how to read a card, 23

I

I Ching, 110

India, 18, 42, 106

Influential Person Spread, 87

inner child, 17, 77, 175, 178, 181, 184

inner teacher, 90–92

introvert, 63, 65–66, 80, 149

Italy, 5, 41–47, 107

J

journal, 3–4, 12, 26, 50, 70–71, 91, 94, 118, 132, 135, 141, 158, 164

journaling, 138

Journey through the World of the Tarot Court (exercise), 48

Judaism, 46, 110, 129, 133, 248

Jung, Carl, x, 65–66

Jungian psychology, 71, 73–74, 76, 87, 245, 248, 249

K

Kabballah. See Qabalah

Kazakhstan, 42

Kazanlar Tarot, 21

Keirsey Temperament Sorter, 66

Keywords, 3, 23, 64, 83, 137–141, 146–147, 160–162, 167

king, 9–10, 16–18, 73–77, 103, 106. *See also* Thoth knight

King of Cups, 28–29, 31, 47, 50, 59, 76, 82, 98, 118, 125, 136, 139, 142, 214, 228, 230

King of Pentacles, 77, 82, 125, 220, 228, 232

King of Sword, 21–22, 47, 57, 73, 77, 86, 98, 116, 125–127, 136, 142, 217, 228, 231

King of Wands, 47, 53, 57, 59–61, 73, 76, 98, 123, 125, 211, 228–229

king archetype, 76

King, Warrior, Magician, Lover: Rediscovering the Archetypes of the Mature Masculine, 75

knave, 46–47, 247. *See also* knight

knight, 9–10, 16–17, 73–74, 103. *See also* Thoth knight, prince

Knight/Prince of Cups, 6, 28–30, 47, 51, 86, 98, 125, 140, 142, 158, 190, 228, 230, 238

Knight/Prince of Pentacles, 73, 80–81, 122, 125, 148, 196, 227–228, 232, 240

Knight/Prince of Swords, 47, 51, 98, 122, 125–126, 144, 193, 227–228, 231, 239